CATALYST CONTENT

How to Create *a* World-Class Piece *of* Thought Leadership *in* Less Than 10 Minutes *and* Leverage *it* 99 Ways

JANE ANDERSON

Copyright © Jane Anderson 2020

ISBN 978-0-6480489-6-1

All rights reserved. No part of this book may be reprodcued or transmitted in a
form or by any means, electronic or mechanical, including photocopying (except und
the statutory provision of the Australian Copyright Act 1968), recording, scanning
by any information storage and retrieval system without the prior permission of tl
publisher.

CONTENTS

01
Why content matters... 1

02
The Top 10 Barriers to Creating Content ... 15

03
What is Catalyst Content ... 30

04
Ideation ... 60

05
Creation ... 79

06
Distribution ... 103

Acknowledgment

I wrote my first blog in 2010 when I started my business. I didn't really know what I was doing but it was a good form of self-expression and it seemed like the right thing to be doing. It was a way for me to educate clients, help people to find me and grow my practice.

Every time I wrote a blog my business got busier and more and more clients came to see me. I thought it was a no-brainer and that everyone was doing it. It turned out that it wasn't. Since then I have had countless conversations encouraging people to create content to not only help their businesses grow but also to help others gain insight into their problems and understand how the business owner can help solve them.

The power of one piece of content can be transformational. It can change someone's perspective. It can change a business. It can even change a life. I've since learned that one piece of content can also be repurposed and leveraged to use across multiple platforms.

There are so many people who have helped me in my content creation journey that I would like to thank. First and foremost is Matt Church, the founder of Thought Leaders Business School and the Pink Sheet Process that I mention in this book.

Learning his process gave me a way to channel my ideas and stop them racing around in my head with no home to go to. Being able to unpack ideas and content effectively has truly been life changing for both me and my clients.

A special thank you to Thought Leaders Business School CEO Peter Cook for his advice and guidance along the way.

Secondly, to all the mentors who have guided me in my content and thought leadership journey including Gabrielle Dolan, Janine Garner, Corinne Amour, Donna McGeorge, Emma McQueen, Lisa O'Neil, Dan Gregory, Keiran Flanagan and Trav Bell. Special mention to my good friends and masterminders Keith Abraham, Rowdy McLean and Amanda Stevens.

Thirdly, thanks to my amazing clients, suppliers and practitioners who inspire the programs I create and books I write. I'm beyond grateful to have the dream practice and tribe of amazing people I get to work with every day. Special thanks to my Business Manager Sam Bell. Also thanks to Lauren Shay, Kristen Lowrey and Sylvie Blair for your publishing and editing support. Final thanks to my family, especially my parents and fiancé, Mark, who are selfless in their advice and support.

Thank you to you the reader for making this book possible!

1

Why Content Matters?

"Content Marketing is the only marketing left." –
Seth Godin

Content marketing is the only marketing left. Yet, we still struggle to implement content that creates engagement and drives change in our businesses and practice. That is where this book comes in.

In Catalyst Content, we're going to meet this need for content marketing head on. As thought leaders, experts, business owners and entrepreneurs, it is essential that we get our messages out to our audiences. We'll discuss the barriers that stop us from doing just that. Then we'll talk about the actual process of content creation, from ideation to distribution.

But most importantly, we'll dive deep into the processes, systems and mindsets that help you take your content from noise lost in the internet abyss to **catalyst content**, that is not just heard, but repeated, and that helps you to truly embrace your role as an expert, a thought leader and a changemaker in your industry.

But first, let's talk about why content is important.

Why does Content Matter?

In late January 1998, then US president Bill Clinton, gave his infamous speech about his dealings with a White House intern, 22-year-old Monica Lewinsky. The scandal had rocked Clinton's reputation, and in that speech he stated, "I did not have sexual relations with that woman." We now know he was lying, and with that statement came a watershed moment – that a prestigious authority, a president, would lie.

Around the same time, the internet became accessible to the public. Suddenly we had access to so much more information (and misinformation), and the way people consumed information and made decisions quickly evolved – and continues to evolve.

Today, we can "Google" symptoms when we feel unwell, search for people's background information and find out more about any subject than ever before. This has also created increased transparency. Instead of the media filtering conversations, social media has given the average person a voice.

As a result, we have become aware of others' opinions. This has led us to question "whom do I trust?"

==Content helps us understand whom we can trust==

Old Trust	New Trust
Certificates	Results
Networks	Reputation
Testimonials	Reviews
Transactions	Tribes
Products	Humans
Popular	Connected
Marketing	Education
Perfect	Authentic

©Jane Anderson

When trying to identify whom we can trust, we no longer look for certificates on walls. We look for social proof, such as an online presence and customer reviews on Google and Facebook. We're trying to find out who has the real influence, the real power and is the real deal.

As a result, leaders and businesses have moved away from formal ways of building trust to far more socially connected and socially proven methods of building trust.

We're living in a digital-first world

In his book *Ctrl Alt Delete*, *Mitch Joel* discusses the term "digital first". He reveals the five fundamental movements organisations must embrace to future-proof themselves – or risk going out of business. One of these shifts is the fact that now, the first place your brand and business are validated is online. The internet has the power to make or break your chances of success.

Serial entrepreneur, Gary Vaynerchuk, is an excellent example of how to cultivate a successful business by leveraging digital media. Born in the Soviet Union in 1975, Gary Vee, as he's known, immigrated to the United States in 1978. From those humble beginnings, his father went on to own a liquor store in New Jersey.

In the early days of the digital-first world, Gary Vee could see the vast potential of his father's business. After graduating from college, Gary Vee transformed the liquor shop into a retail wine store, which he named the "Wine Library". In 2006, he started a daily video blog, *Wine Library TV*. This hugely popular webcast turned him into an internet celebrity. It attracted 90,000 viewers a day and led to a flurry of TV and speaking engagements. In just six years, Gary Vee grew the family business from $1 million a year to a whopping $50 million a year!

As you can see, traditional marketing has been blown out of the water. We're no longer restricted to cold calling and setting up meeting after meeting to generate leads and sales. Digital marketing has opened an array of cost-effective avenues for self-promotion and lead generation. Sales are now about leveraging your social networks, engaging with people online and educating.

This is, essentially, the social sales model:

Past	Present	Future
Employees	Role Models	Ambassadors
Cold Calls	Tribes	Engagement
Sales Demonstrations	Education	Thought Leadership
Salesperson	Trusted Adviser	Expert
Transaction	Solution Selling	Lifetime Partnership

© Jane Anderson

Today, the businesses and entrepreneurs that make the most impact on their audiences are role models. They're trusted advisers who create tribes – powerful online communities that help their brands grow. They educate and provide solutions. They've jumped on board the social sales train and have embraced the connection economy whole-heartedly. Because if you don't embrace change, you get left behind.

But, as leaders, we can't rest on our laurels. We must build on this massive sales reform and look to the future. We must become trusted industry ambassadors; thought leaders who engage meaningfully with our followers, share generously our expertise and regard our audiences not just as leads or dollar signs, but as lifetime partnerships.

Sometimes though, we struggle to get out content. It can, at times, seem like there's so much content out there already, and just so much noise, that it's hard to keep up. It can seem like it's impossible to make our own message heard. But the data disagrees. People are consuming more content than ever, and we're producing less.

People are consuming more content than ever

The data tells us that people are actually consuming more content than ever, but we're creating less content than the market can consume and less than we have in the past. This is particularly true in Australia. We're starting to pick up, but we're not creating as much as other countries like the US.

We've got some challenges in Australia, such as the "tall poppy syndrome". We struggle to put ourselves and our ideas out there for fear that people might see us as believing we know best or are "better than them". But the reality is we need to be a tall poppy – we need to be seen.

Content marketing is a major growth industry. In 2015, the content marketing industry was a $118 billion industry. In 2021, the content marketing industry is expected to be a $421 billion industry. That is extraordinary growth. People are starting to capitalise on this growth, recognising that content marketing is the key to getting in front of clients. We need to be doing the same.

Business growth in a social-first world

Business growth today works quite differently to how it used to work years ago. It used to be about cold-calling, sales demonstrations and qualifying leads. But today it's all about engaging and educating your social media audiences. So, first we ask the question, 'who do you know and who knows you?'

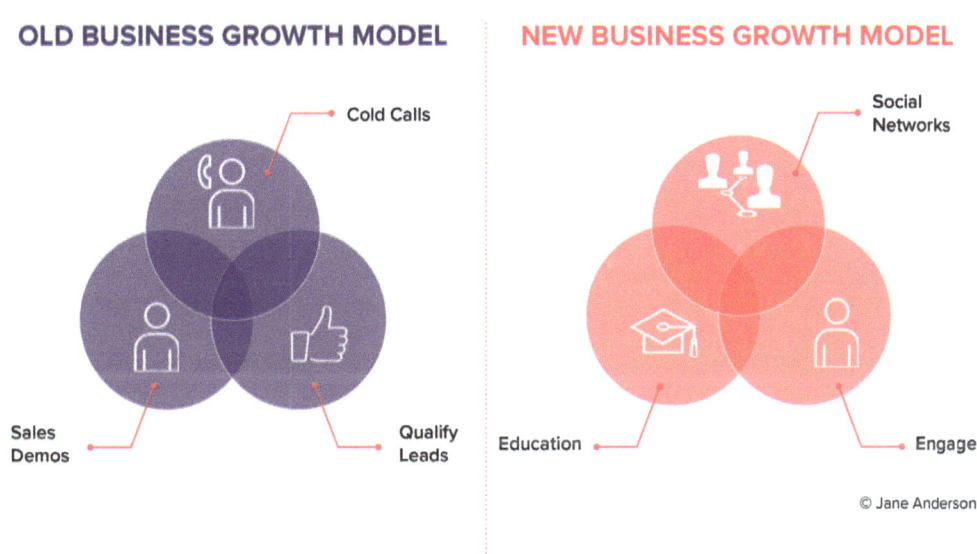

The second thing we've got to work out is now that we know who you know, how are you going to educate them? You can't simply get in front of people and keep contacting them over and over. That's called spamming. And if you keep sending them sales emails they're just going to unsubscribe. You've got to find a way to add value and help them, and the way to do that is to educate them. You've got to teach them.

The third thing we need to do, once we've worked out who we know and how we're going to educate them, is engage. Our content is the vehicle for doing that.

We need to move our target audience out of the information super highway in order to engage them to come and work with us in our businesses and practices. The data shows that this works. In fact, content that educates increases engagement by 83.6%[1] . That's a big jump, and a big way to get attention and prove to your audience that they can trust you to bring value into their worlds. Create content that's not noise. As *Seth Godin* says, "The world doesn't need more cat videos". What the world needs is change, and it's our job as change agents to give voice to that.

The whole point of content marketing is to help you build a tribe, a community of people who have a leader, a message and a way to communicate. So, if you're going to build a sustainable business, you need to build a tribe and a community of people around your message. Remember, you can't sell a secret. You have to actually share your message. You have to repeat it over and over again. You have to find new ways to make it interesting, and break it down into really simple messages that people can understand.

Dunbar's Metrics

Robin Dunbar, who's a social anthropologist, tells us how to do this using data he calls 'Dunbar's metrics'. His research focused on indigenous tribes in the Amazon and Australia, among other places, and asked, "What is it that makes those tribes sustainable? Why have they survived through so many thousands of years, when other tribes have died out?"

1Stebbins, C. (2017). "Educational Content Makes Consumers 131% More Likely to Buy [RESEARCH]." Conductor Spotlight. https://www.conductor.com/blog/2017/07/winning-customers-educational-content/

Dunbar's metrics are numbers that identify the levels in your tribe. It starts with the number five. Five is the intimate, really close group around you. It might be your family, or very close friends. The next number is 15. In the tribal setting, 15 is your tribal council. For you, it's your board of directors or your board of advisors. These are people who have your best interests at heart and who can help you grow your business. So, they might be mentors, or it could be people in your team, your accountant or even your business coach.

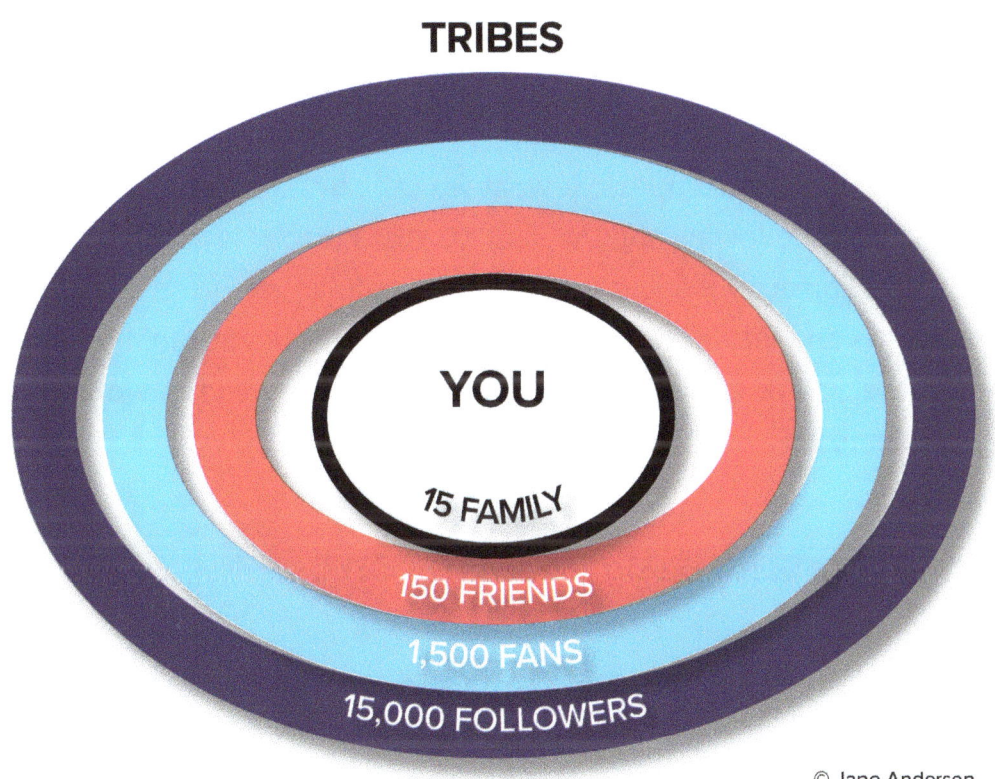

The next layer in the Dunbar metrics is 150, and this is the data Dunbar is best known for. He's identified that people who are leaders or experts in a field, only have enough bandwidth for about 150 people. Most people and businesses have far more contacts than that on Facebook alone. So, to grow our practice we've got to learn to look after and nurture our top 150 clients. They've looked after you by spending money with you. Your job now is to look after them.

Matt Church, the founder of Thought Leaders Business School, calls the the next layers out the fans and followers. The fans are the people who are on your database and who are opening your newsletter every week. This number is about 1,500. These are your fans who are ready to listen to your message but aren't, perhaps, your top clients.

Finally, the last metric is what we call our followers. This is your social media following and the goal for that number is around 15,000 people. Ultimately, we want to move those followers from our social networks and into our database. And once you've got them on your database, you've got to nurture them. You actually need to work with your database and the inner tribe.

What is Catalyst Content

In order to build your database, and engage, educate and nurture your tribe, you need to create the right kind of content. The model below helps illuminate what catalyst content really is, and how it works.

1. Invisible

At the lowest level you're putting content out but you're still essentially invisible. You're on platforms, but you're not getting any traction. So the first thing you've got to build is a sense of connection. You've got to work out, "Who am I trying to help? Why am I here?" Get really connected to who you are, and what it is that you know, and what you would like to contribute to the world. At the lowest level you have no leverage, which is what you need to be successful. And because you have no leverage, you're probably losing market share and very quickly.

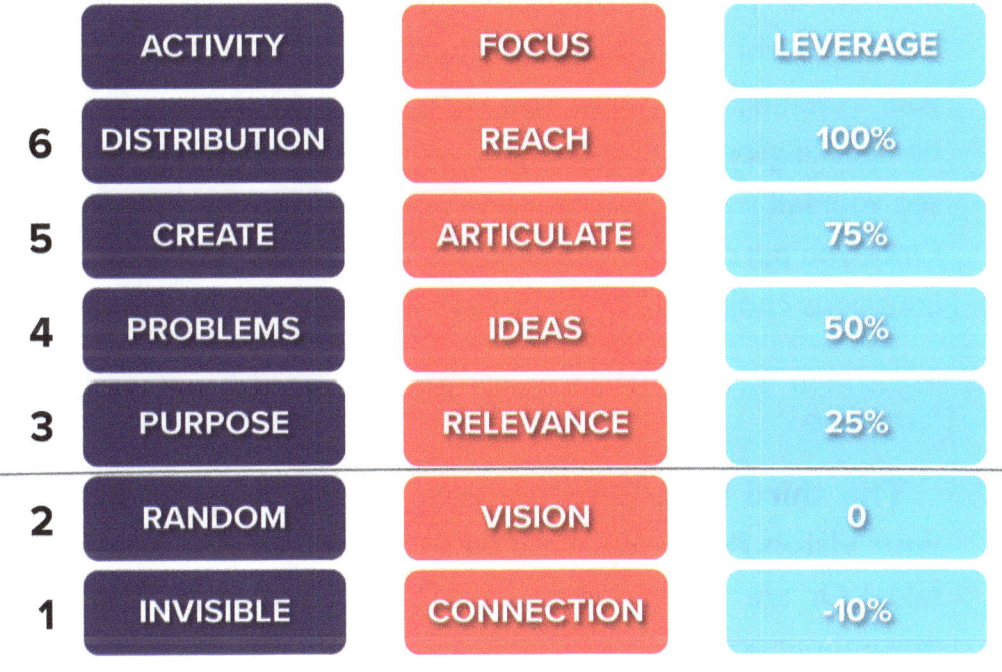

2. Random

At the second level, most people are putting content out but without focus. This type of content feels random and disorganised. They might have photos of their lunch, and pictures of their dog, which is then followed by a thoughtful post about the economy. It's quite a mix, and for some people or in some situations, that's actually OK. It's OK to share aspects of your personality. In fact, it's a good thing. But when you're an expert in your field you have to be really on message. You have to be really consistent with what you're trying to say so you don't pull your audience all over the place.

At this level you need a really clear vision. You have to know what it is that you're actually trying to create. What is the business or practice of your dreams? Who is it that you love working with? What are you actually trying to do in terms of your revenue? Where do you want to work? Do you want to be speaking on stages? Do you want to be coaching? Do you see yourself traveling all over the world or working from home? Once you pin down your vision, then you can start making some conscious choices about what you're trying to do.

3. Purpose

The third level is to understand the purpose behind your vision. Are you trying to create sales? If so, how many sales? Or are you trying to build brand awareness? Maybe it's more about positioning. Once we are clear on the purpose of the content, then we can focus on its relevance. So, we can tailor it for our audience and their specific problems. This takes us to the fourth level.

4. Problems

The fourth level is all about relevance and audience. Now, we focus on the problems people have so we can start creating content around the solutions. It's not about saying, "Here are all the solutions that I have in the world, and here's what you should be doing." Some might call that a crusade. Instead we need to offer empathy. We've got to put ourselves into our audience's shoes and say, "What are the things I'm struggling with? What questions do I have? What am I afraid of?"

Once we've worked out relevance, we can start to create solutions that are meaningful and practical. And you'll be able to connect with your audience. Remember the golden rule of personal branding – it's not about you, it's about others.

5. Creation

The next level, level five, is capturing and unpacking your solutions. This is where we articulate all the pieces that make up the solution to each problem. And to do that, we've got to tell stories. Well-researched stories that give practical steps.

6. Distribution

The last level is about the distribution of that content. If we can get our content out to a broad audience of our ideal clients, then it's leveraged to its absolute potential.

The big goal

People sometimes try to get too much happening on social media, but social media is where you need to start. It's the best place to add value and connect with people who will eventually become part of our tribe. And it's the best place to help our tribe grow.

It's really important that we understand the goal from our catalyst content, and therefore this book, and that is to build a tribe. We're trying to build a community of people around our message, and the only way that we can do that is to create the content.

This book

This book will guide you on your catalyst content journey. It'll take you from where you are right now to where you need to be. Catalyst content isn't just pretty memes and cat videos. It's content that sets you apart as an expert and drives change. And driving change is your job. It's your job to set people up for the future of work.

At the end of this book you'll be at a point where you're capturing your ideas, articulating your message and distributing your content to increase its distribution and reach. That will help you leverage your content into catalyst content.

2 The Top 10 Barriers To Creating Content

Many years ago, I divorced and started life over again. I had five years on my own to build my business and focus on what I needed for a while.

Once I was back to a level of independence, I decided to start dating again. It was hard, as so much had changed. How people met had changed, how they communicated had changed, I was older, and, suddenly, I felt a bit washed up. Admittedly, I was only 39, but I don't think I've met anyone who hasn't been daunted by the experience of putting themselves out there again.

I think it's the same for the clients I work with. As we start unpacking their expertise and knowledge, it can be quite daunting. An element of vulnerability goes with sharing what you think, sending it out to the public in a newsletter or online. It looks easy until it comes time to do it. We hit a wall of self-doubt, avoidance and fear. We worry we won't be good enough or that we don't have the time – endless excuses and fears that hold us back from being fully self-expressed.

Creating content is a vulnerable process and, yes, I was in the same boat when I started. I questioned who would listen to me, if I was relevant and what I could possibly share that hadn't been shared before. But once you know how to overcome these barriers to creating content, it's like turning on a tap – the ideas start pouring out, and a weight lifts off your shoulders. Having helped people create content for the past eight years, and writing my own blog for the previous 10, I have found people commonly face the following challenges:

1 I don't have time

There's no doubt about it, we're all trying to do more with less. We're overwhelmed by the sea of noise, the barrage of emails and social media updates, not to mention the demands of everyday life. Trying to get to the gym, go to meetings, look after family, have a life outside of work… all these things add up and we can't seem to find the space and time to create.

So, how do we find the time to create? The first thing to do is ask yourself whether you can see the connection between creating content and what you're trying to achieve. If you have a business and you know you need to create content to get more clients, but you're not creating, then do you really want to run a business? Or do you want an expensive hobby?

Equally, if you're a leader and don't have time to write content, what is your purpose? The role of the leader is to drive change. How can you drive change without communicating? How can you make time to reach out to people and connect with them if you don't see the value of creating content?

The second part to this is that you may not have found the cadence and rhythm of unpacking your ideas. This comes from deciding what your days, weeks, months and years will look like so you can create content. For example, I have several female business owners who are also mums come to my Content Creation Bootcamps to get away from their daily distractions and get focused. We create 12 months' worth of content in two days. Other people catch their ideas on the run, capturing and creating content in moments. Others create content in batches – for example, once a month or week. Others do it first thing in the morning.

> It's up to you to be conscious and pay attention to how you work. Don't try to be perfect, but identify what allows you to make progress. It's time to buy yourself some "bum glue", remove all distractions and get focussed. As the adage says, "Time is money," and every opportunity you miss to share your ideas means fewer clients, less influence and less change.

2 My ideas aren't good enough

Everyone faces the challenge of feeling like an imposter – even the most seasoned experts and Content Creators. The benefit is that everybody else is afraid of the same thing. You have a massive advantage if you face this challenge head-on and take action. Because if you don't, the consequence is inertia, which means nothing changes. You continue to feel like your ideas aren't good enough, that your accomplishments come from luck and that you're a fraud, and you don't create content.

One of my clients, Jess, went through the same experience. Jess was a young mum who felt like she could help people, but she wasn't unpacking her ideas. She didn't think they were good enough; she felt like an imposter. But once Jess unpacked her ideas and started sharing, she got swamped.

In fact, she became so busy, she had to force her prices up. She even won a "mumpreneur" award!

> Author *Maya Angelou* once said, "I've written 11 books, but each time, I think, uh-oh, they're going to find me out now. I've run a game on everyone and they're going to find me out."

How do you overcome this fear? You need to do the work. Start unpacking your ideas and get your knowledge out of your head and onto paper. The more you create, the more you build your confidence.

3. I have nothing to add. Everything has been said.

The difference here is you. You have a different world view, different experiences and different knowledge. The context you operate in is completely different to everyone else's, and this adds substance and insight to what you say.

When you think this way, you're also only considering those who are searching for information, which is just 25% of the market. It's like handbag designer *Kate Spade* saying, "Well, there are already *all these handbags out in the world, what value could I bring?"* Tell me, what woman wouldn't want a new handbag just because she already has one!

What's more, if you look at the amount of content people are creating on LinkedIn, it's quite small. Only about 1% of people are creating content, and the research tells us we're consuming more than we are producing, especially in Australia. The market hasn't been able to keep up.

Don't become someone who isn't meeting the demand for content. Focus on what you need to do. Stop looking at everybody else and focus on your clients, your tribe and being their leader.

4 Can't I get somebody else to do it or outsource it?

Yes, you could. However, your content wouldn't be you. People would see through it.

It's important your ideas originate from you, at least. You can get help to unpack the rest of it and do some research, but you need the ideas to come from you. Otherwise, your content can seem a little like Weekend at Bernie's – it's got the sunglasses on, trying to pretend it's you. After a while, people will work it out.

19

> If you need to outsource content, at least be interviewed by the person writing your content. You can go online and purchase content cheaply, but it becomes inauthentic, and you will commoditise yourself. Bought content and articles are super vanilla and boring. People want your insights and ideas, and these are what set you apart.

5 What if I get trolled?

The word "troll", which comes from a fishing term, is internet slang for somebody who starts arguments, upsets or harasses people by posting off-topic or extraneous messages. They're like a school bully – they might be picking on you, but what they want is attention.

Huffington Post recently shared some research that said of 1,125 adults, 28% admitted to malicious online activity directed at somebody they didn't know. My experience has been that it's much less than this. Perhaps these results were due to a high volume of bullies in a particular group?

I do love this quote from stand-up comedian *Dane Cook*. "Trolls look for reasons to hate but really what they are mad at is the fact they are not included in anything ever."

Most of the time, it's generally best to ignore the trolls or not care. It says more about them than it does about you.

6 Fear of being boring

The reality is, most people share this fear. No one wants to be boring. The key is to stay visible and know how to add value to your audience.

Saying you don't want to be boring, so you just won't share content, is a bit like saying, "I don't want to go to the supermarket, so I just won't eat."

The best thing about regularly sharing content is that it becomes part of your every day. It also validates other people. By seeing and hearing from you frequently, by being part of your every day, your audience gets to see the real you – not just the best bits. This enables them to relate to you more, and they start to connect with you at a human level.

A great way to **overcome the fear** of being boring is to get started. Share your everyday-type situations – but also make sure you share your insights. And if you fill out your content form in the upcoming chapters, then you will create something that's definitely not boring.

Justin Timberlake once said, "The most boring thing in the world? **Silence**."

So, the more frequently you can create, the less boring you will be! And remember, people connect with real, not perfect. Engage with your audience by asking questions, creating videos, using memes or creating a podcast with your content. There are so many different ways to engage people. The only way you'll bore people is by saying nothing – or sharing cat videos or photos of your food every day!

7 I don't know how to use technology

Great. You're not the only one. Technology changes every day on some platforms. As soon as I wrote my book, Connect, about LinkedIn, it was out of date. The goal is to stay in your genius – you're not a technology expert.

Working with some technology can make you feel like you're in a foreign country. It's like a completely new language, and you have to re-learn it all the time.

> *George Couros*, author of The Innovator's Mindset, said, "Technology will not replace great teachers, but technology in the hands of great teachers can be transformational."

Using technology as a leader to inspire and communicate with people, to lead them through change, is truly transformational. Don't let this overwhelm you. Keep it simple. You may even need to ask for help from administrative staff or others in your organisation, or a virtual assistant if you're running your own business.

8 I don't know what to create.

One of the challenges we face is that we don't know what to create. The reality is, you have great ideas all the time. You know how to solve your clients' problems; your solutions are perfect. You just need to capture these ideas and solutions.

> I remember when I felt like I didn't have anything to share and didn't know what to create. But then I followed the process of writing my ideas down. Over time, it became a habit, the ideas flowed more freely and creating content became much easier for me to do. Now, I've written seven books. If you had asked me five years ago if that was possible, I would have laughed!

One of my clients, Naomi, also didn't know where to start or what to create. So, we simply got started. After she wrote her first blog, she got a roadshow for speaking at five events around the country. As you can see, action really does precede clarity!

9 What if I say the wrong thing and upset someone?

How often do we say things or do things in the normal course of our week that other people may not like or agree with? Content creation is about showing up and taking the lead on a topic. And we know that leadership often means doing things that feel uncomfortable.

I love this quote from *Martin Luther King, Jr*, "A genuine leader is not a searcher for consensus but a molder of consensus."

What if people disagree? That's great news. If we all had the same thing to say in life, it would be boring.

The reality is, you don't get anyone to agree with you if you stay silent. It doesn't mean you have to be disagreeable. By sharing your ideas, you help your audience to gain a greater sense of self. Whether they agree or disagree, they get more insights into themselves.

Aristotle once said, "It's the mark of an educated mind to be able to entertain a thought without accepting it."

I often think of the book Above the Line by *Michael Henderson*, culture expert for the New Zealand All Blacks.

He said, "If you want to go to a greater sense of who you are, have lunch with somebody you don't like."

> It's the same thing for your audience. Giving people a greater sense of themselves is one of the greatest gifts you can give. It means there is a higher purpose to your content, and you're giving your audience more insights.

The more you can get clear on who you are and who you're not, the better you'll become as a leader. You'll cut through.

> *Russell Brunson*, in his book, Expert Secrets, talks about polarising experts. **He says,** *"Those who are at the extremes of polarisation will actually have higher levels of people who don't like them or don't agree with them, but those who are in the middle actually are the ones who are least able to connect with people."*

Push the edges a little if you can. If people disagree with you, try not to take it personally and always thank them for their opinion.

10. It needs to be perfect.

10/10

One of the most common things that holds people back is the idea that content needs to be perfect. People compare their initial drawing, note or scribbled thought to a published book or blog, and believe that what they've created should be of the same standard.

There is no such thing as perfect. And there is no such thing as immediately creating something perfect.

This was a big lesson for me as I started creating my content. When we look at a published author, we can trick ourselves into thinking this incredible genius must have sat down and immediately created a masterpiece, with no need to edit, spellcheck or proofread. It simply popped into their head and onto paper in perfect form.

Many of the clients I speak to don't realise that an author's ideas were initially scrawls or scribbles on a piece of paper, just like theirs. The writer then went through the process of unpacking their mess of thoughts. They researched, wrote drafts, had their work copy-edited, proofread and typeset. There is a process from capturing an idea to distributing it – the content doesn't just magically appear. Who would have thought!?

As *Margaret Atwood*, author of The Handmaid's Tale, said, "If I waited for perfection, I would never write a word."

Questions for you to answer

1. Which of the barriers hold you back from unpacking and sharing your ideas? Is it one or more, or all of them?

   _____

   _____

   _____

2. Why does this or these hold you back?

   _____

   _____

   _____

3. What is the impact of this holding you back? Money? Revenue? Cashflow? Time? Influence?

   _____

   _____

   _____

4. What advice would you give someone else struggling to overcome this barrier?

_____
_____
_____

5. Is the belief you have around this barrier actually true? What would be a more helpful belief to adopt?

_____
_____
_____

6. Based on what you've learned in this chapter, what will you do to overcome that which holds you back?

_____
_____
_____

7. How will you implement this?

_____
_____
_____

8. Who can you ask for advice on overcoming this block?

_____

_____

_____

9. How will you celebrate?

_____

_____

_____

10. What strategies will you implement to make this sustainable for you?

_____

_____

_____

3

What is CATALYST CONTENT

"We don't need more content. We need better content."
Ann Handley

Catalyst content is not just noise. It's content that builds brands, engages customers and leads and drives change.

There are three key areas that will help you to create enough content for your social media platforms, newsletters, internet platforms and more. The three key areas are *ideation, creation* and *distribution*.

Ideation

Ideation is the process of coming up with ideas for your content. Some of the key questions to answer are:

1. What are the ideas that you want to share?
2. Which ones are commercially smart and link to your business goals?
3. How do you capture those ideas?
4. What tools are you using to store and catalogue those ideas so that you can use and repurpose them?
5. What do you do to improve your ideas? How do you curate and aggregate the ideas of others to extend your own thinking and the thinking that is out in the world?

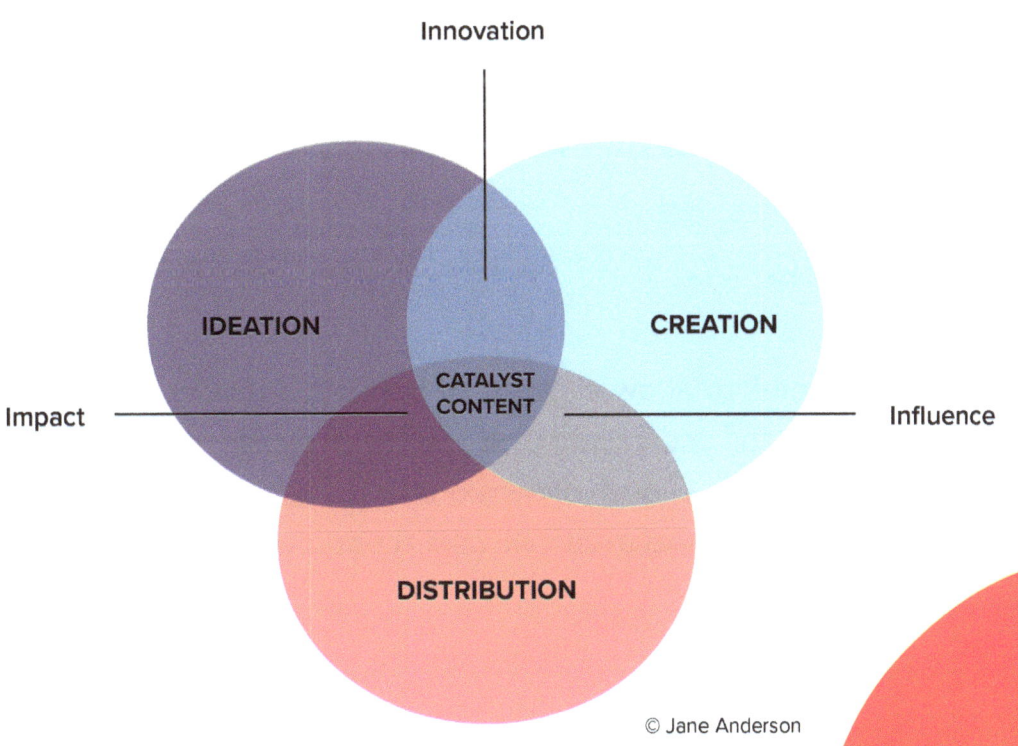

Creation

Creation is about how you create the content for your ideas. It's not enough to simply write one line, send it out to your audience and expect them to take action. Before you send content out to your audience you need to really think about what you're trying to say. And you need to find enough ways to say it so people understand.

A fully formed piece of content should include many different angles and methods to get your message across to your audience.

This includes aspects such as:

- Storytelling;
- Research;
- Having an opinion;
- Quoting others;
- Recommended steps for taking action;
- Metaphors; and
- Models.

You need to show a depth of thinking, consider how your audience learns and understand their specific challenges and problems for your idea to have enough dimensions to it. Then you can influence them to change their behaviour or take action.

Distribution

Distribution is how a piece of content is moved out of your head and into the world. This is where people often get a little stuck. They don't always know how to leverage an idea to its potential and optimise the reach that it can have.

Years ago a website was the only platform for your content. You'd post it and just hope that people would find it. But today, one piece of content can be leveraged across multiple platforms using a variety of media. In fact, there are around 40 different ways and platforms content can be leveraged. This includes:

- Website
- Newsletter
- Podcast
- A chapter in a book
- LinkedIn update
- LinkedIn article
- Facebook Live
- Instagram Stories
- Instagram TV (IGTV)

And this is just the start!

Whether it's used in podcasts, presentations, videos, written posts or infographics, it's essential you keep track of the content that is distributed. So having good systems in place to manage your content is key.

Catalyst
Content

At the intersection of ideation and creation is **innovation.** It's the place where we're constantly driving forward. Where we're consistently improving and finding ways to advance our thinking. We're no longer at the peril of disruption. Instead, we become the disruptor.

At the intersection of creation and distribution is **influence.** It's here that we start to get our ideas in front of people and people start to do what we want them to do. Whether it's buy more products, sign up for our webcast or come to our next event. If we want them to be more vulnerable, or authoritative or mindful of how they do something at work or how they get through change, this is where we start. We're changing the narrative and, in the process, changing what people think.

At the intersection of ideation and distribution is **impact.** It is here where our ideas and the ways that they're distributed start to get the results that we're looking for. If we're trying to get change, if we're trying to get revenue, if we're trying to get leads — whatever the outcome is that you're trying to achieve, this is where the actual results start to happen.

You don't want to be creating content for content's sake. It needs to be content that is created and that actually get results. And if you can get the results, then you're far more likely to continue to do it. You're also far more likely to value your ideas and the impact that they can have.

How to
Leverage One Piece of Content 99 Ways

My grandfather was a pastry chef. He passed away when I was 16, but one of my most abiding and treasured childhood memories is going with him to the bakehouse in the very early morning. Lamingtons, an Australian specialty, were one of his specialties – in fact, his lamingtons were out of this world.

Making the days' worth of lamingtons was an intensive process. He started with massive slabs of vanilla sponge cake, that were cut up into squares with a large cutting form. Each tray of cubed sponge was then dipped in thick, luscious chocolate before being covered in flaky coconut.

Each baking day my grandfather made something like 1,000 lamingtons in a single go. As a child I was always impressed by the sheer volume of deliciousness he created every day. But now I understand that this was the best way to get the highest return on your investment.

If my grandfather had prepped and cooked each lamington individually, it would have been a far more labour and time-intensive undertaking. And, it likely wouldn't have been worth the effort.

Creating content is much the same. When you create a single piece of content, and use it for a single blog, or one Facebook post, you are wasting time and energy. A much better approach is to take one piece of content and leverage it into many, many more. In fact, you can take one piece of content and leverage it into 99 separate pieces of converting content.

Why
you should leverage your content

Leveraging content is not about using the same thing over and over in a boring repetition. It is also not about creating more digital noise. There are three important reasons to leverage your content.

1. It maximises your resources.

When you leverage your content you are maximising your resources. This one piece of content stretches your time and your money to give you maximum impact for the least amount of input.

Business owners are busy, and we simply don't always have the time or even mental energy to be composing content every single day. Leveraging gives you an opportunity to create valuable content with less effort.

2. Content has a short lifespan.

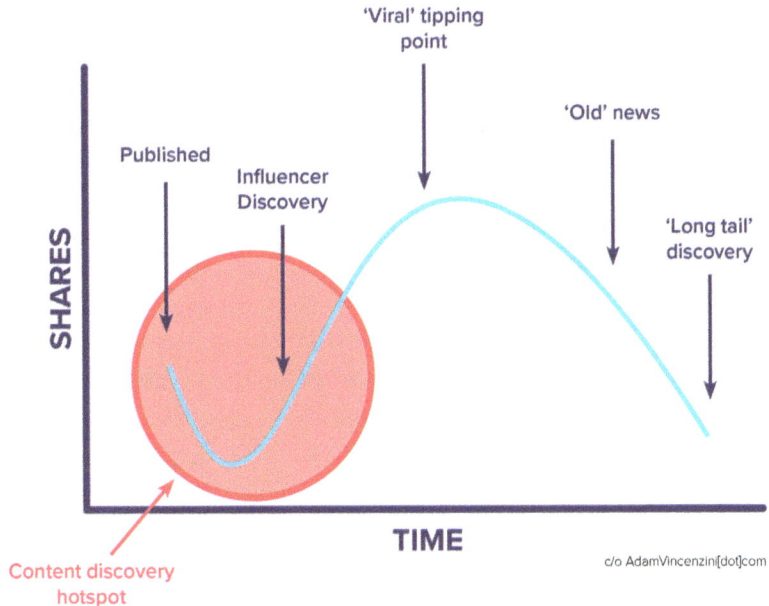

As you can see from the model above, content has a short lifespan. And different platforms have different useful lives.

IT company, Mamsys[1], conducted research about the lifespan of content. They found that a blog post lasts for two years, a Pinterest post for four months, YouTube videos for 20 days, LinkedIn posts for 24 hours, Instagram posts for 21 hours, a Facebook post has about five hours of visibility and a tweet on Twitter has a lifespan of roughly 18 minutes.

Creating content is a way to keep your audience engaged with your brand. But you have to keep creating it. Regardless of the platform, it doesn't last forever.

---

1 Lifespan of Content Model. Mamsys, [Date]. https://www.mamsys.com

3. It's how you reach your community

When you leverage your content you're effectively meeting people where they are and distributing your content in the learning styles they like. For example, some people prefer Facebook to LinkedIn, and some will prefer Twitter to IGTV. When you create content on each of these platforms you are meeting people where they are comfortable and where they like to hang out online.

In the same way, some people prefer to get information via the written word. Others prefer to watch videos or listen to podcasts. If you can access each of these different methods then people can 'learn' from you in the way that best suits them.

Leveraging & Distributing Content

But how do you actually do it?

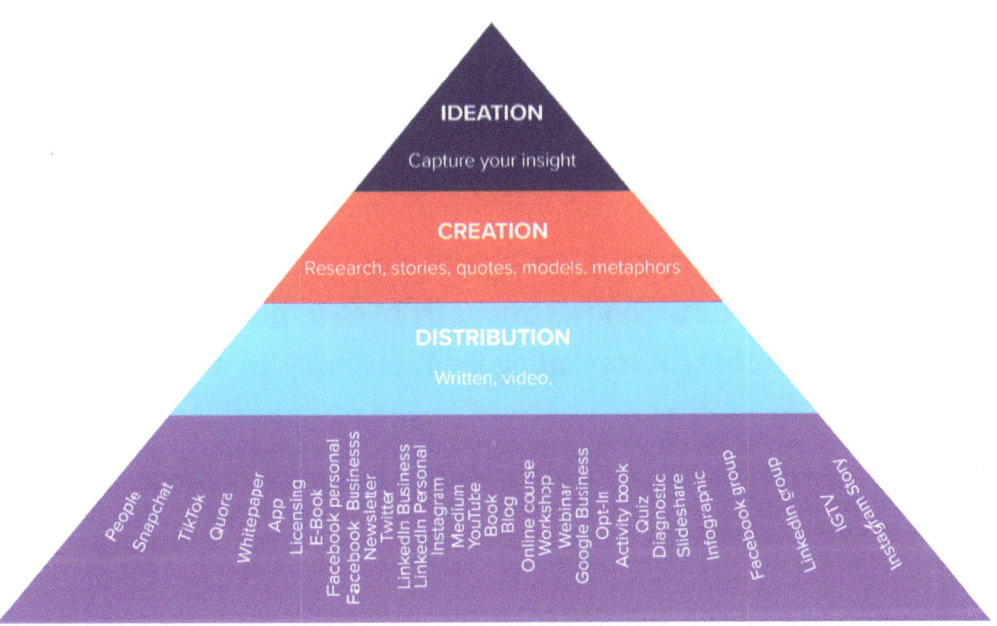

First you get your great idea (ideation), then you think about your written, audio and visual approaches (creation) and then you'll distribute your content through multiple channels (distribution).

The model above shows 33 different channels of distribution starting with people (or face-to-face interactions) and ending with Instagram stories. Of course, there may be others that are particular to you or your industry – perhaps an industry conference or a masterclass. And there may be some that suit your business and audience better than others.

But the more distribution channels you can access, the better your chance of reaching the right people. And your 33 options become 99 when you take advantage of the written, audio and video streams as well.

Note about efficiency

At the end of the day, leveraging your content is more about being an efficient manager of your content than it is about being creative. The creative process takes place first but the rest is just plain good business management.

Like my grandfather's lamingtons, content leverage helps you get the highest return on investment from each piece of content. It can move your content marketing from ordinary, to extraordinary.

> 'The hours that ordinary people waste, extraordinary people leverage.'
> – Robin Sharma

What
type of Content Creator are you?

One of the issues I've found when helping to create their content is trying to identify the type of Content Creator they are. Having a level of self-awareness and how you work can have a big impact on the amount of content you create.

I recently worked with Megan, who came to work with me at one of my Content Creation Bootcamps. Before the bootcamp, she said, "I'm really struggling to get my newsletter out. I want to write my book, but I just feel like I've lost my creative mojo. I feel like I don't have any ideas anymore. I've exhausted everything I can think of."

Megan felt so depleted, she was worried she would leave the bootcamp with no new ideas. So, I asked her to identify which type of Content Creator she thought was. This was so we could put together a strategy so that when she came to the bootcamp, she would be 100% ready to create 12 months' worth of content in two days.

We all have a natural cadence and flow when it comes to creating content. Knowing your natural style will help you generate more ideas. It will also help you improve productivity, become more prolific in your content creation and make better decisions about how to get your content in front of people so that you can grow your influence, impact and income.

By creating content, you put yourself ahead of the game. This is because not enough people are doing it! In fact, only 1% of people on platforms like LinkedIn create content.[2] There are more than 500 million LinkedIn users, yet only three million of them create content.

So, while it may seem like there's a lot more content on LinkedIn these days, there isn't. User content creation has been at this 1% rate since the platform began. Now that we have algorithms to compete with, we must be more strategic and targeted with our content to get the most from it.

In today's world, we deal with cognitive overload. The problem is that most people are struggling just to get work implemented and maintain the status quo. This reduces their creativity and ability to create content.

We're also dealing with a lot more noise. As a result, it's becoming harder for the average person to innovate, come up with ideas and create content to ensure those ideas have influence.

---

2 Osman, M. (2019). "Mind-Blowing LinkedIn Statistics and Facts (2019)." Kinsta. https://kinsta.com/blog/linkedin-statistics/

However, if you are prepared to put in the effort, be prolific and create content, you give yourself a significant advantage. You will have the greatest influence.

As *Donald Miller*, author of Building A Story Brand, says, "The only people who influence culture, after all, are the creators."

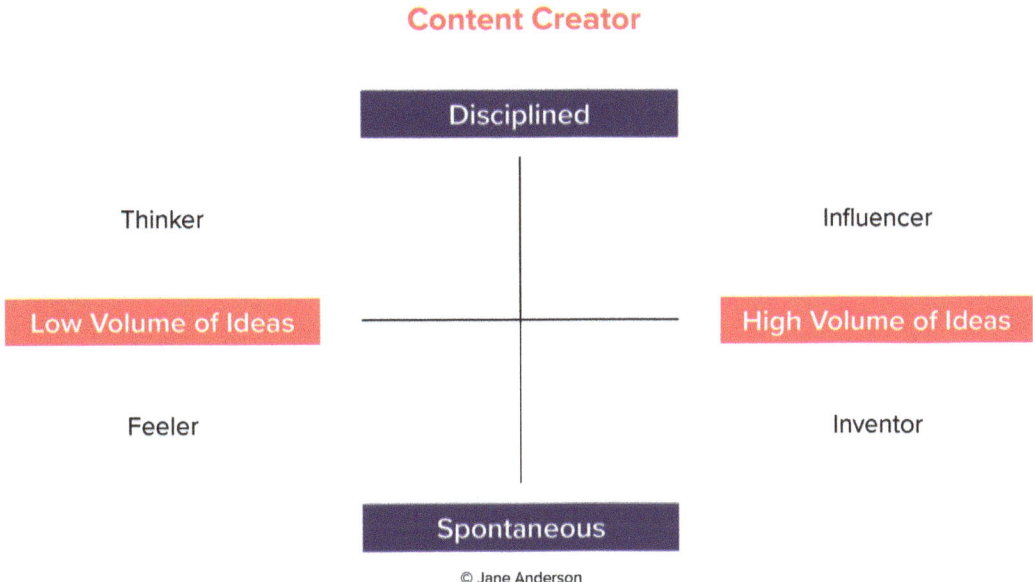

To be a prolific Content Creator who has influence and impact, you first need to understand your Content Creator type. Are you an **Influencer, an Inventor, a Thinker or a Feeler?**

The Influencer - Steve Jobs

Influencers have a high volume of ideas. They are able to find a balance between the organisation of these ideas and their creativity. They're like a Steve Jobs. They ensure they capture their ideas, use tools to create less work and block time for execution. They're deliberate, intentional and harnessed in their approach, and are unafraid to fail their ideas fast and quietly.

Their advantages

Influencers realise that perfectionism is the enemy. They are not concerned about each piece of content being "just right". They know that creating high volume and being on message allows them to go deep with their communications and become prolific.

Influencers treat their content creation process like a conveyor belt. It's a process that continually flows through their practice, with idea generation moving to creation to distribution with ease. They know what parts of this process they can delegate, and what parts they need to do themselves. As a result, they don't suffer from creative blocks. They're present to their ideas, and they prioritise their content creation in a way that works best for them.

Influencers understand they need to create a high volume of content to get to the really good stuff. As Jobs said, "That's what makes great product. It's not process, it's content."

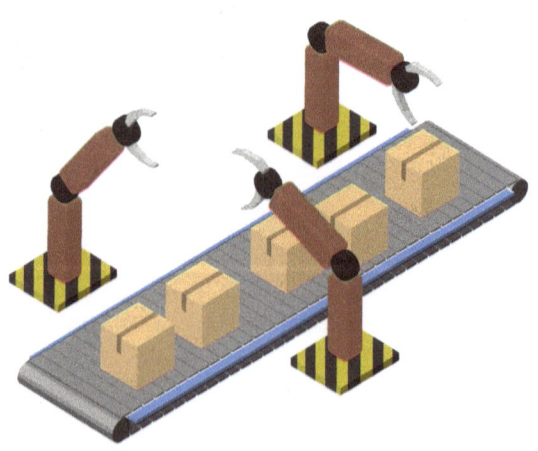

How:
Influencers
can optimise your content creation.

The Influencer's advantage is in being **strategic and disciplined.** Their challenge is to open themselves up to new and unexpected experiences to create deeper insight. Rather than simply reading others' content, they're making a creative space to apply their lens to other contexts.

Look for the fun, meet people you wouldn't normally spend time with, read books you wouldn't usually read and go to places you wouldn't usually visit. Try to find different ways to disrupt your mindset and different ways of asking yourself, "What do I think about this?"

The Inventor - Albert Einstein

> **The Inventor** comes up with ideas all the time. They're fully present to the amount of ideas they create and they value their thoughts, ideas and interpretations.

Their advantages

Inventors are prolific in the amount of IP they create. They're like an **Albert Einstein.** Einstein created more than 50 patents. He constantly looked at the world around him and tried to find ways to improve it. For example, he didn't have a five-year plan to create the Einstein refrigerator; he simply noticed that people needed a better way to keep food cold, and so he created the patent.

> The difference between today and the early 1900s is the advent of distraction. The Inventor in all of us struggles to be present to and capture ideas because we're constantly distracted. Social media, texts, phone calls, interruptions in open-plan offices – the list goes on. We're switched on 24/7. Einstein could focus far more easily than we can today because he didn't deal with the same distractions.

How:
INVENTORS
can optimise your content creation.

The challenge for the Inventor is to ensure they maintain focus. Generally, they're naturally creative and disciplined people. But they do need good systems in place so they can capture, create and catalogue their ideas and content. This may mean turning off technology for an hour or even a few days at a time to do deep work on their content. Apps like Memo Mailer are useful for capturing ideas on the run.

> As *Einstein* said,
> *"Creativity is intelligence having fun."*

The Th!nker - Hamlet

In Act 3, Scene 1, of Shakespeare's Hamlet, the protagonist says, *"To be or not to be, that is the question."* Hamlet was the classic overthinker, although his challenge was more about obsessing. Obsessing has a circular narrative – it goes around and around. Similarly, thinking does not always follow a linear narrative and can stop people from progressing. Thinkers often say to themselves, *"I just need time to think,"* but they don't make the time.

These Content Creators tend to overthink everything and have a perfectionistic approach to unpacking their ideas. They worry too much about what others think, and they're often stuck in the paralysis of analysis, dwelling on a situation for so long that they can no longer act.

Their advantages

Thinkers are adept at creating a space where they feel safe. This improves their confidence in the short-term and maintains the status quo. Once they identify a process that allows them capture their thoughts, they spend less time in their head and more time sharing their ideas and content.

How:
TH!NKERS
can optimise your content creation.

Thinkers need to unlock their ideas with a daily cadence and rhythm that creates new neural pathways for creativity. In the short-term, I recommend making a list of the top 20 things they know about in their area of expertise. Doing this for just one week helps them make the shift from thinking to doing, which results in generating more ideas to gain traction and momentum.

The Feeler - Homer Simpson

One of TV's most loved characters is **Homer Simpson.** Homer likes to do the least amount of work with the least amount of effort. He is a man of leisure and doesn't do anything he doesn't feel like doing.

> One of his famous quotes is,
> *"If something's hard to do, then it's not worth doing."*

Their advantages

Feelers tend only to create when they feel like it. Like Thinkers, the advantage is that they remain safe. They don't lose energy and they maintain the status quo while waiting for their moments of genius to arrive.

Another, less obvious advantage is that Feelers often have valuable insight into what stops people from taking action in their area of expertise. They're so close to the problem and can articulate the issue in greater detail than almost all other Content Creator types. Being aware of those insights and seeing them as valuable is key to their content creation. Otherwise, the assumption is, *"Isn't that everyone's issue? How is that even helpful?"*

How:
FEELERS
can optimise your content creation.

Feelers need to focus on two areas to unlock their creativity and content creation: cadence and empathy. Quite often, Feelers face challenges around the *"imposter syndrome"*. *"I don't feel like I have any good ideas,"* is a phrase commonly said by Feelers.

Letting go of perfectionism is also valuable. Feelers can feel hopelessly unoriginal, as though it's all been said before. They have a fear of looking incompetent and must overcome their need to be liked. They're often not used to asking for help, and their self-talk is about not being good enough. They are excellent procrastinators and tend to avoid creating content because of how they feel about it at that moment, instead of thinking about the long-term benefits of having influence and leading change.

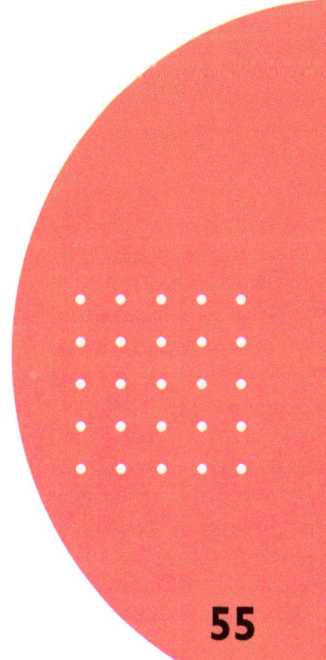

WHAT CONTENT CREATOR TYPE ARE YOU?

By identifying your Content Creator type, you will be able to channel your ideas, become prolific, make a greater impact and wield more influence as a change agent.

> As creativity expert and best-selling author *Elizabeth Gilbert* says, "Creativity is a crushing chore and a glorious mystery. The work wants to be made, and it wants to be made through you."

What type of Content Creator are you? What strategies do you need to put in place to become more prolific in your content creation?

Questions for you to answer

1. What are you thinking about creating content on?

   _____

   _____

   _____

2. How will this help your audience?

   _____

   _____

   _____

3. How will this content help you grow your business or influence as a leader?

   _____

   _____

   _____

4. Where are you gaining your ideas from currently?

_____

_____

_____

5. How are you capturing your ideas currently?

_____

_____

_____

6. What process are you following to create content currently?

_____

_____

_____

7. How are you leveraging every piece of content right now?

_____

_____

_____

8. What holds you back in your ideation, creation and distribution?

　
　
　

9. Which of the Content Creator types do you resonate most with and why?

　
　
　

10. Once you've determined the type of Content Creator you are, what strategies will help you create more content?

4

IDEATION

"A man's mind once stretched by a new idea never regains its original dimensions"

Oliver Wendell Holmes

In his bestselling book, *Blink: The Power of Thinking Without Thinking*, US journalist Malcolm Gladwell describes artists who are charged with the job of determining whether a sculpture is a fake. Those considered experts each had more than 10,000 hours experience examining genuine art and were able to identify the fake art in the blink of an eye. Gladwell contends that 10,000 hours is *"the magic number of greatness"*.

In other words, establishing your thought leadership requires a huge investment in time and practice. It also means having a thorough understanding of your strengths and skills, and the ability to capitalise on them.

My client Michelle is a great example of this. Michelle was the property manager for a family that owned 18 buildings in Brisbane. Her job was to train the family's daughter to take over the business. Michelle came to me feeling unfulfilled, believing there was no career progression for her. But she also didn't know what other kind of job to look for. Looking through Michelle's resume, I noticed that most of the roles she'd had previously started in business development or sales, then turned into training roles.

After undertaking the Myers-Briggs Type Indicator® assessment, Michelle discovered she had an ENFJ personality type – Extraverted, Intuitive, Feeling, Judging. ENFJs are natural teachers and leaders who inspire others to better themselves. Michelle had been an educator for most of her life, even though she might not have called herself that. After looking at all her achievements, her story and her expertise, it was clear that Michelle was all about giving people the chance to achieve their potential.

When I pointed this out to her, she became teary. No one had ever said that to her before. She had never been clear on her true strengths, skills or passions. Michelle realised that she had spent so many years doing what she was good at, but not what she loved.

She was now free to do what she wanted to do in a different space, using her hard-earned 10,000 hours – her thought leadership – for a higher purpose.

Know your strengths and your weaknesses

Thought leadership is key to becoming an Influencer. It's what you want to be known for. Remember, it's not good enough to simply know something – you want to **be known for knowing something**. So, if you're a little unclear on your thought leadership, you need to work out your strengths.

How can you do this? A simple way is to do an assessment of your strengths. We often find it easier to identify our weaknesses. But to move forward and take responsibility for the direction of your life and career as an Influencer, you must be able to identify both your strengths and weaknesses, and then amplify the strengths you possess.

We all have something that sets us apart from others. To start understanding your strengths consider the following:

- What are your advantages?
- What do you do well?
- Why did you decide to enter the field you are in?
- What motivated and influenced you?
- Are they still part of your inherent strengths?
- What need do you expect to fill within your organisation or position?
- What are your most notable achievements?
- What knowledge or expertise will you bring to your business and clients that may not have been available to them before?
- What is your greatest asset?
- What has led to your successes?

Ultimately, your personal brand and positioning as an Influencer begins with you. Until you know yourself better, you can't effectively convey who you are to anyone else. By singling out your strengths, passions and expertise, and being honest with yourself about your weaknesses, you will find clarity and focus. It will enable you to share your knowledge and elevate your thought leadership.

Some questions for you to consider as you reflect on your strengths and weaknesses:

- If you woke up tomorrow with an ideal life, what would it look like?
- How do you want to be remembered? What would the speech at your 80th birthday sound like?
- How well positioned are you to ask for what you want in your salary or fees?

Once you are clear on your strengths and the key messages of your thought leadership, you can start to position yourself with a content plan. In 2014, $135 billion was spent on content marketing[1]. It is set to become a $420 billion industry by 2021[2].

This means that organisations and customers are buying your authenticity and your brand. Brands who are the most authentic are the most bought. We cover content marketing in more detail later in the book.

---

1 "20 Captivating Content Marketing Facts in 2014," Jeff Bullas. https://www.jeffbullas.com/0-captivating-content-marketing-facts-in-2014/#mPy71V53BSrk04KZ.99

2 "Content marketing will be a $300 billion industry by 2019," Marketing, July 10, 2015. https://www.marketingmag.com.au/news-c/content-marketing-will-300-billion-industry-2019/

As *Steve Jobs* said,

> "Focus and simplicity is one of my mantras. Simple can be harder than complex. You must work hard to get your thinking clean to make it simple. It's worth it in the end, because once you get there, you can move mountains."

Your thought leadership makes you unique

Thought leadership is a bit like notching up the kilometres on your car. It's not necessarily the type of car you drive – in other words, the kinds of jobs you've had – that matters. It's your accumulative experience, the skills you've gradually built and consistently used that count.

> **If I looked at your work history,** what's the common thread in all the roles you've had? Where have you been? What have you done? How do your experiences add up to create your unique thought leadership?

We all have a lens through which we see the world. Thought leadership is making this lens visible and valuable to others. Consider how others can learn from your thought leadership.

How can it benefit them so that they buy from you? Essentially, it's about clarifying your mastery. Your thought leadership must make an impact on the world.

In fact, thought leadership is not only desirable but essential if you want to survive in business. By 2020, 50% of the workforce will be self-employed[3] . According to South African futurist and strategy consultant Dr Graeme Codrington, the people who know how to market and brand themselves for the future will be the ones who survive.

And to do that, you must be able to unpack your insights and understanding. This has been identified in the Future Work Skills 2020 Report as "sense-making".

We are increasingly living in a world of knowledge workers – people whose job it is to think for a living. In Australia, four out of five people are employed in a service-based business. This isn't going to change any time soon.

So, to grow this type of business and succeed in this era of knowledge workers, you must be on top of your content.

It takes 10 pieces of content before somebody decides to work with you, and 90% of that decision is made before they even get in touch with you. Sharing your thought leadership is key.

Shelley Barrett, CEO of cosmetics brand ModelCo, says to succeed, it's essential that you truly understand your industry. "When I went into business, I thought I was going into the world of beauty, when in actual fact I was going into the world of retailing, wholesaling, marketing, logistics, finance."[4]

---

3 "The Rise of the Freelancer Economy," *Forbes*, January 26, 2016. https://www.forbes.com/sites/brianrashid/2016/01/26/the-rise-of-the-freelancer-economy/#103efc593bdf

4 ModelCo founder Shelley Barrett shares her two best pieces of business advice," *Mamamia*, November 11, 2015.

One of the greatest challenges for industry experts and thought leaders is to make sure their message and expertise can be bought easily.

Creating a message you're passionate about is one thing. Making sure that message has a buyer and can generate an income is another. It's important to be clear on the actual problems you solve so your product or service is monetisable.

Once people know how to buy you, you can differentiate yourself from the rest. But if you try to be too clever by showing off your expertise through throwing rocks at your audience or pointing out their failures, you will repel your market.

They might not even understand what they're buying from you. Know the category you're appealing to with your thought leadership so you stay on message and make the most impact.

What's your category?

Here are some sample categories of how expertise and branding are bought across public and private markets:

Thought Leadership	Corporate Category	Public Category
Organisational Futurist	Culture Leadership Futurist	Leadership
Personal Branding	Communication Marketing Leadership Influence Confidence	Communication Marketing Leadership Confidence
Lifestyle Strategist	Productivity	Weight loss Work/Life Balance
Intrigue Expert	Storytelling Communication Influence	Communication Marketing

©Jane Anderson

When sharing your message, you need to link it to the programs, products or outcomes that you're trying to create. If, for example, you're trying to sell your management consulting services, then all your content needs to relate to the aspects of management consulting that you help people with.

Equally, if you're within an organization and you're trying to lead people through change, then you as a leader need to share messages that are in line with that change. So, for example, I've recently been working with a large global multinational's "people" team. To accomplish their goals, they needed to be posting once a week on their internet platform, Facebook Workplace, to drive their core messages around helping people through change. Some of the aspects that they're sharing are things like resilience, mindset, purpose, self-care and adaptability, for example.

When you can get your messages right, it's a bit like having a compass. It tells you the direction that you're going, and it keeps you focused to make sure that the content that you're sharing is narrow and concentrated on the outcome that you're trying to achieve. It stops you from confusing the audience and ensures that you stay focused on the best way to create influence.

According to research undertaken by Google it takes between 20 and 500 touch points to take a possible customer to a customer that is ready to buy from you[5]. That can be a mix of face-to-face and online communication.

Years ago, Robert Cialdini wrote the book, *Influence: The Psychology of Persuasion*. And his research found that it was five to seven touch points. But the research today tells us it's much, much more than that, because we're having to compete with so much noise.

When you're trying to work out what messages you need to share, think about what specific programs you're selling? What are the messages that go with that? These messages can be created around educating, providing information or setting out solutions to problems.

---

[5] "Why It Takes 7 to 13+ Touches to Deliver a Qualified Sales Lead (Part 2)," *Online Marketing Institute*, October 24, 2013. https://www.onlinemarketinginstitute.org/blog/2013/10/why-it-takes-7-to-13-touches-qualified-sales-lead-part2/

My advice to you is to just grab a clean sheet of paper and write down 50 messages that you would like to share.

So, for example, if you wanted to share something around customer service, then you might consider using the following messages: how to deal with refunds, how to greet people, how to increase your add-on sales, how to go the extra mile or how to deal with customer complaints, for example.

There are three key steps to help you identify your key messages. First you need to identify the brand and the essence of who you are. Think about the personality of your brand, what is your unique value proposition and what are the programs or products that you're trying to sell. In this step you're really identifying who your business is, or who you are if you are an expert in your field.

Second is to identify the themes within your brand that match what you're trying to sell. For example, if you're trying to sell the concept of change, what are the themes and messages within change that you want to send? So, it might be about resilience, or leadership, or personal responsibility or even mindset. All these themes, or key messages, about getting through change are vital. Being able to know what you need to unpack in relation to what outcome you're trying to achieve will help you identify your themes.

The third step is capturing ideas. Really good ideas often come along at really bad times when you're not ready or not present to capturing that idea. The reality is, is that you're solving problems all the time. You're working with your customers to solve the challenges that they're facing every day.

You're constantly sharing and advising, and these are all pieces of content that you're creating every single day.

The problem is that you're not always mindful of or present to what you're saying. As a result, you don't necessarily see the value in those pieces of content because it's just stuff that you do every day. You need a system and a process to capture these moments of brilliance and inspiration as they're happening. If you don't do this, you will have so many lost opportunities and even though you will be allocating time to sit down and unpack your ideas, those ideas might not be there when you need them. You need the system and the knowledge to be able to put them into blogs, books, podcasts, interviews and content for your internet platform.

Ideation for catalyst content requires speed and volume. The benefit of knowing how to unpack your ideas is that you will become prolific at creating, clarifying and distributing your ideas through your content.

If you don't know how to begin with ideation, you will procrastinate. You will create friction in your creative process, losing time and reducing your output significantly.

Why is ideation so important? **Your ideas** are like the foundation of a house or the legs on a table. They are what support and strengthen your brand. You need to get your ideas onto the conveyor belt so they can be processed and distributed through your marketing and communications channels.

There are **three levels** to establishing effective ideation for your IP:

1. Spark your ideas.
2. Seize your ideas.
3. Store your ideas.

Spark inspiration for your ideas

Many people find they hit a creativity limit and struggle to generate ideas. They worry and complain that their ideas have all dried up, but in reality, they just haven't found a way to let their creativity flow.

It's a bit like turning on a tap. You need to find a way to turn the tap on for your ideas. Most people are surprised to find that when they discover how to turn their tap on, it stays on – it's no longer a matter of turning it on and off.

> As *Pablo Picasso* said,
> *"Inspiration exists, but it has to find you working."*

Leonardo da Vinci, renowned for painting the Mona Lisa and inventing the bicycle, had no formal education, yet he was a genius at generating ideas. He was influenced by his uncle, who loved nature. Da Vinci was an artist and an architect, and he talked about making the most of random, chance events to produce variations in thinking patterns.

He advised people to contemplate clouds, pavements and walls, to be present and take notice of the things around them. He said it was important to theorise and make connections between everyday things to find inspiration and create new ideas.

There are many ways you can spark inspiration and turn on the tap for your ideas. One way is to increase the amount of reading you do. This expands your knowledge base and introduces you to new ways of thinking. You can also watch movies, travel, attend sporting events or listen to music. The point is to seek a variety of experiences to help spark and tap into the ideas within you.

Seize your ideas

Thomas Edison once said,

"To have a great idea, have a lot of them."

Elizabeth Gilbert, in her book, Big Magic says that our ideas are like monkeys and we need to capture them.

If we don't, then they're likely to just jump away. What we have to do is grab the monkey by the tail and not let that monkey go anywhere until we have a home for it.

There have been times where I've delivered programs in training courses and caught myself saying something and I have to stop and quickly get it down. In fact, we use a tool called Memo Mailer, which myself and productivity expert, Dermot Crowley, created to capture ideas and get them down really quickly. You can go onto iTunes or Google Play and download it for free.

If you imagine, it's a little bit like a mental defrag. If you capture the ideas as you're going, you can speak them into your Memo Mailer and it will send an email capturing the idea. Then, once a week, when you have the time allocated to process those ideas and actually create them (we'll talk about this in the next chapter), then the idea is ready to be unpacked. So you have a conveyor belt of IP, and each is moving onto the next logical step of your content creation to help you to create an impact.

It's imperative that you have the capacity to capture your ideas all the time. Use the ideas we discussed, like Memo Mailer or another note-taking app. Remember, seizing your ideas is about grabbing hold of them quickly so they can be retrieved and unpacked later. But you need to be attuned to those ideas and have the right processes in place to seize them.

Store your ideas

Even if you're not ready to unpack your ideas yet, you must store them so they can later be developed, distributed and can start generating revenue, income and influence.

Your ideas are life. They can't be left to wither and die. You need to put them onto a conveyor belt to be processed, ready for production and distribution. As *Richard Branson* once said, *"Ideas are the lifeblood of business. Capture every fleeting idea and drive for change."*

Matt Church, founder of Thought Leaders Business School, explains some data on the value of an idea versus a fully formed idea. Research we undertook in Thought Leaders Business School shows that, on average, the value of a fully formed idea for a thought leadership expert is around $10,000. So, once you start to realise your ideas are assets and can add significant value to your practice, you will begin to prioritise their creation and look after them.

One of my clients, Renee, is one of the most creative people I know. She continually has ideas and creates a lot of content.

But one thing she really struggled with was having a system and process in place so her IP could be stored for easy retrieval, reference and repurposing. So, we implemented business process mapping.

Created by the American Society of Mechanical Engineers in 1921, business process mapping is a way to visualise what a business does by taking into account its roles, responsibilities and standards, to improve efficiency and workflow. When it comes to ideation, the client maps their practice or business (or, for leaders, their role within an organisation) to ensure not only that their ideas are stored properly, but that their entire business function is mapped correctly. The result is that their idea files match the different parts of their business and are managed the same way.

Business process mapping is a simple process, but it is the world-class standard in gaining efficiencies in your practice. So, how does it work? First of all, you put yourself in the centre, then work out all the pieces of your practice – e.g. finance, marketing, content creation, running programs, delivery, sales. Then, you create a folder for each business area (you could use Dropbox, Google Drive or another online file-storage service), so that as your ideas appear, you simply upload them into the relevant folder.

Kerry Gleeson, in his book, *The Personal Efficiency Program*, talks about being able to map your job for maximum efficiency and productivity. Mapping – understanding the features and functions of something – really is the foundation of all efficiency, and it's what will ensure you capture and process your ideas.

Questions for you to consider

1. When you think of your "10,000 hours", what words come to mind?

   _____
   _____
   _____

2. What do you see as the greatest hurdles for people in their roles at work or in their lives?

   _____
   _____
   _____

3. What frustrates you about people or the world?

   _____
   _____
   _____

4. What do you think would make people happier, more engaged, more productive and more conscious?

_____

_____

_____

5. When have you actively disagreed with something or someone?

_____

_____

_____

6. What do you wish you'd known that you found out the hard way?

_____

_____

_____

7. What advice do you repeatedly give to others, such as your team, your manager and your family or friends?

_____

_____

_____

8. What was something that you found difficult to learn?

9. What do you get referred for? What skill or task attracts people who need help to you?

10. What aspect of your thought leadership might be missing in your branding?

5

CREATION

"Life isn't about finding yourself, it's about creating yourself."
George Bernard Shaw

It's not enough to simply come up with an idea. You need to develop your idea into something tangible, something that can be learned, understood and acted upon by your audience.

Now, you might think you didn't get the creative gene when you were born. I used to think that, too! However, after writing seven books, I can tell you there is a process you can follow to unpack your ideas effectively, even if you aren't particularly creative.

There are lots of different ways to unpack your ideas that add value to your audience. I have been a mentor and on faculty in Thought Leaders Business School, where I mentored experts to help them unpack their ideas and knowledge. **Matt Church**[1] , founder of Thought Leaders Business School and author of *Think*, teaches something called the **pink sheet process**[2] . This process offers a simple and effective format to tap into the context and content of an idea. Going through this process forces you to get into the habit of balancing your head and your heart in your content.

As Buddhist monk *Thich Nhat Hanh* once said,

> "The longest journey you will ever take is the 18 inches from your head to your heart."

I think he's right. It is vital that you balance your head and your heart in your content because around half of our audiences are heart based and the rest are very head based, so the balance is key.

Elle Geraghty has also created what is called the **Content Canvas**[3], which is a tool to measure the metrics of a piece of content. This tool, and others like it, can be useful as more advanced tool for more experienced Content Creators once you have had a go at starting to create content.

---

[1] Biography of Matt Church, Thought Leadership [online]. Available at https://www.mattchurch.com/about.

[2] Pink Sheet Process [online]. Available at https://www.pinksheetprocess.com/.

[3] Geraghty, Ella (28 February 2019), "Content Canvas PDF" [online]. Available at https://www.ellegeraghty.com/blog/2019/content-canvas-pdf.

In this book we're going to start simply yet with high impact to create content that catalyses change. We're going to use a tool called your "Content Page".

CONTENT PAGE

#	Key Message			
Opinion e.g. Benefits, Consequences etc				

Story	Research	Quote	Metaphor	Steps

© Jane Anderson

CONTENT PAGE

# 1	Key Message	Getting through the highs and the lows
Opinion e.g. Benefits, Consequences etc	When we go through change, it's not smooth sailing. We experience ups and downs do things we've never done before. It can feel slow and laborious.	

Story	Research	Quote	Metaphor	Steps
Story of me moving to new town as a HR Advisor, Didn't know anyone, new tasks, new people	Carol Dweck Growth Mindset Book and Ted Talk on her research	"Test Scores and measures of achievement tell you where a student is at, they don't tell you where a student could end up." Carol Dweck	Like a roller coaster	1. Reflect on how far you've come 2. Focus on your strengths and celebrate small wins 3. Tomorrow is a new day, take the opportunity to reset

© Jane Anderson

Story

In your Content Capture, you start with story. You need to captivate your audience. Simply giving your audience step-by-step information on what to do will bore and exhaust them. You need to capture their attention through storytelling to inspire, engage and motivate them.

Seth Godin said,

> "People do not buy goods and services, they buy stories, relations and magic."

Indeed, research shows that content with stories increases the retention and visibility of that content. **The Financial Review's Boss Magazine**[4], said storytelling was one of the keys to the future of workplace communication and will continue to be, particularly for executive information.

Stories are like a direct connection to the heart. The problem is, quite often, our content is trying to get to the brain.

In her book, *Hooked,* Gabrielle Dolan describes the story one leader told his team. When he was a child his mother used to make him eat Brussels sprouts, which he hated. He would pick at them on his plate and they would go cold, even though his mother would tell him to eat them first to get it over and done with. The leader used this story as a metaphor for the Monday morning sales meeting. He

---

[4] Walters, Kath (14 February 2014), "Once Upon A Time' [online]. Available at https://yamininaidu.com.au/wp-content/uploads/2016/04/Financial-Review-Boss-Magazine-Storytelling-article-14-Feb-2014.pdf.

was, in essence, asking his team to just get it over and done with. Needless to say, his story stuck within the team and the organisation. This is because it's both a personal story and a metaphor that is relatable and easy to understand.

Star Stories

There are five stories that will typically help you with your business communication. I call them STAR stories:

- ◆ **Personal story**: Something that's happened to you – typically, a hero's journey, as described by writer Joseph Campbell.

- ◆ **Inspirational story**: An inspiring story about yourself, a client or somebody well known.

- ◆ **Case study**: Typically, an example of somebody you've worked with.

- ◆ **Historical story**: A story of somebody from history who's no longer alive.

- ◆ **Metaphorical story:** This is where the story contains a lesson or metaphor for the point you're trying to make.

These STAR story types can interrelate and connect – they don't have to be mutually exclusive. For example, you could use an inspirational story that is also a personal story, or a metaphorical story that is also a historical story.

Research for Credibility

Your content needs to position you as an authority, expert and leader in your field. And as a leader, credibility creates trust, which, in turn, creates influence.

Senior consultant from FranklinCovey, Shawn Moon, talks about the four cores of credibility:[5]

- Results
- Opportunities
- Intent
- Integrity

Moon says that competence sits above the surface and is visible to others, while character, like the roots of a tree, is under the surface and isn't noticeable.

For our content to be credible, we need to share both our competence and our character. That means we need to be able to share those things that are invisible to our audience. We can create a narrative to share our character and competence and so increase our level of credibility in our content.

Aristotle said we need to include three key areas or "rhetorical appeals" in our content to ensure we are influencing and persuading. These are:

◆ **Ethos:** Who can you reference who supports your claims and who your audience respects and admires?

◆ **Logos:** What documentable evidence, such as research, data or statistics, supports your claims?

◆ **Pathos:** Creating an emotional response and empathy by telling a convincing story.

---

5 Moon, S. (2017). "Trust Starts With Who You Are" [online]. Available at https://www.linkedin.com/pulse/trust-starts-who-you-shawn-moon/.

Remember, your title doesn't mean you have influence. The question is, are you getting results in your work and team? What level of respect do you have currently? If you are finding you're slow to gain traction with your credibility, you need to work hard on your positioning and communications.

Use the three prongs above to support your content. Make sure it's backed by authoritative references (ethos), peer-reviewed evidence (logos) and elicits an emotional response (pathos). That's how you build credibility.

And, in the words of leadership expert *John Maxwell*, "Credibility is a leader's currency. With it, he or she is solvent. Without it, he or she is bankrupt."

When we're sharing our content and IP, we need to ensure we have a purpose and a reason for it. You need to tell your audience what you want them to do next – your call to action (CTA). If you don't make this clear, they will do nothing, and the value in your content is lost. You must have a purpose behind what you share.

In his book *Jab, Jab, Jab, Right Hook*, Gary Vaynerchuk explains that "jabs" are the lightweight pieces of content that benefit your customers by making them laugh, snigger, ponder, play a game, feel appreciated and escape. Right hooks are calls to action that benefit your business and what you need to ask for, or what you need to sell.

Call To Action

Gary Vee says sharing content is like boxing. You have to create lots of little punches, before you can go in and deliver the right hooks. Otherwise, your opponent will just duck and head for the hills. They won't stay to engage with you any longer.

This strategy applies to your content. You need to ensure your content delivers lots of jabs followed by strong right hooks. Your CTA is that strong right hook.

A call to action is the icing on the cake. Essentially, it's a clickable link, button or image that prompts your readers to act. If you've given your readers informative, compelling content, by the time they reach the end of your post, they should feel inspired and motivated. Don't let them read and run. Ask them to act on their motivation.

Be clear and specific about your call to action. What would you like your audience to do? What is your objective? For example, you may want to build your client database. If so, provide a button that links to your newsletter opt-in form. If you have a book you want to sell, direct your audience to your shop. If you want readers to sign up to a workshop, create a button that links to your registration page.

Make your call to action as **simple and clear** as possible. Your readers will see it as the next logical step and will be more likely to click that button.

Some examples are:
- Have an opt-in, so people sign up for something.
- Ask your audience to subscribe to something.
- Let them try something for free.
- Invite them to 'do this at your next team meeting'.

Or you can simply use the following succinct CTA types:

- Learn more.
- Join us.
- Get started.
- Come to an event.
- Book now.
- Register here.
- Buy your ticket here.

A great call to action links your content to your purpose and your ideal outcomes. So, take the time to think about your goal and how that correlates with your call to action. You may decide to have a completely different CTA altogether.

Creating Written, Audio and Visual Content

Since the 1920s there have been multiple researchers and theorists who have discussed how people learn. Over time these experts have identified three key learning preferences, which are:

> **Visual:** the learner prefers to engage via images and words (i.e., reads blogs and views images, memes and photos.
> **Auditory:** the learner engages via sound (podcasts and audio files are preferred).
> **Kinaesthetic:** the learner prefers to engage with the content or prefers movement in the content (videos, quizzes, polls).

Equally there are learners who use a mixture of all learning styles to varying degrees. The takeaway is, in order to reach different members of our target audience, we need to ensure our content uses a mix of media to share our message.

Written Content - Blogging

Blogging is a cost-effective, efficient way to educate people. It engages people with your brand and content, and it is essential for establishing your thought leadership.

Think of it as letting your potential clients take you for a test drive. We've all come across the stereotypical car dealer who only cares about getting their commission. But before we buy, we need to get to know the car. We can't be hurried into a decision. We need to know if it's safe and economical. We need to know if it feels right. How do we do this? We take it for a spin.

Blogging takes your audience on a test drive into your world. It shows them your insights and perspective. It gives them a solid understanding of who you are and what you do. When written effectively, blog posts also act like a mirror – the reader sees themselves and their issues in what you're saying.

As an *Influencer*, you can't afford not to blog. Research shows that marketers who blog receive 67% more leads than those who do not[6].

Furthermore, 81% of US online consumers trust information and advice from blogs, and 61% of US online consumers have made a purchase based on recommendations from a blog.[7]

Write Valuable Content

Regular blog posts are also a fantastic way of boosting your SEO. The more relevant content you have on your website, the more likely you will turn up in online search results. By using your targeted keywords in your blog posts and publishing consistently, you'll have a more viable online presence.

To generate leads and drive customer action, your blog posts must add value. Your audience must walk away feeling as though they have learned something or gained a valuable insight. But sometimes when we are so close to our topic, we fail to look objectively at what we write.

---

6 Allen, O. (2015). "6 Stats You Should Know About Business Blogging in 2015". *HubSpot*. Available at https://blog.hubspot.com/marketing/business-blogging-in-2015?__hstc=191390709.192e8b026871b521aa8678a81e7a2bf8.1481076904054.1481076904054.1481076904054.1&__hssc=191390709.1.1481076904054&__hsfp=1190710965#sm.0001mt00m4myrcr5zso25xv9zvz4i.

How do you know if your content adds value? According to *Forbes*, "if people seek it out, if people want to consume it, rather than avoiding it," then your content is valuable[8]. The idea is to have people coming back for more. You want to create blog posts that people share and comment on.

To ensure your blog posts are engaging, educational and valuable, you need to:

Be clear about your message and your audience.

It's surprising how many blogs have so much to say yet fail to deliver a punchline. What's the point of what you're saying? What's your takeaway message? Who is your target audience and what do you want them to walk away with? How would you like them to act on the information you're giving them? Your message and your audience will also help you determine your tone of voice. Will your message have more impact if it's written in a conversational style? Or should it have a more instructional tone?

---

8 Steimle, J. (2014). "What Is Content Marketing?" *Forbes*. Available at https://www.forbes.com/sites/joshsteimle/2014/09/19/what-is-content-marketing/#2e04f01e10b9.

7 Charles, J. (2016). "10 Important Reasons Why Entrepreneurs Need to Take Blogging Seriously." *Huffpost*. Available at http://www.huffingtonpost.com/jeff-charles/10-important-reasons-entr_b_10964854.html.

Make it unique.

Don't regurgitate the same message everyone else is making. Offer something new. What do you have to say that no one else is saying? What makes you different to everyone else? How can you get your message across by sharing your unique stories and perspective?

Use images.

Enhance your content with photos, illustrations and infographics. The strategic use of images will not only break up the text and make your posts visually pleasing; they can help you emphasise a point and guide your readers through your ideas.

Have a clear structure.

You're not writing a book, but blog posts still need structure. Without clearly organising your content, your message will get confused and your audience will stop reading. Use subheadings, bullet points and regular paragraph breaks to help with the flow of your content. This is also essential for SEO.

Use internal links.

Hyperlink words or sentences that relate to other pages on your website. This not only boosts your SEO, it also encourages readers to linger on your website for longer and consume more content.

And remember to proofread your blog posts. Poor spelling and grammar detract from your message and undermine your position as a respected industry leader. A good rule of thumb is to write your post, edit it, then wait 24 hours before you give it a final proofread. This gives you the clear headspace you need to detect errors that otherwise may go undetected in the rush to get it published.

Audio Content - Create Podcast

Podcasts have been around since the early 1930s in the form of radio shows. The term was first mentioned by Ben Hammersley in The Guardian in February 2004, along with other names for the new media platform. Since then, thousands of podcasts have been created in almost every genre and topic you can think of!

Podcasting creates an intimate way for you to connect with your audience. It brings you into people's lives at a very personal level, as they can't skim content or headlines with audio.

To access a podcast, listeners will generally go to iTunes or Google Podcasts and search for a category or your name. It's an easy, convenient way for people to consume your content. Unlike text and video, a podcast doesn't require the undivided attention of your audience. People can listen to podcasts anywhere – while they're on their daily commute, exercising or in the park on their lunch break – meaning you can reach more people and have more impact with your content.

A podcast keeps things interesting. You can add music and voice-overs, have regular guests and interview experts in your field, which helps with your networking and adds authenticity to your brand. And you become more intimate with your audience while educating them in an informal yet memorable way.

What's more, relatively few businesses do it. This means you'll stand head and shoulders above your competitors.

Here are some interesting statistics as to why podcasting is so powerful for your positioning as an Influencer:

According to the latest podcasting statistics up to June 2019:[9]

- 51% of Americans ages 12 and up have listened to a podcast in the past month. This is up from 17% in 2015. Monthly podcast listenership has increased by more than 75% since 2013.

- The podcast audience is made up of 56% men and 44% women.

- 51% of listeners have a four-year degree or higher, with 41% earning more than $75,000 per year and 21% earning more than $100,000 per year.

- Podcasts are driven by mobility. When podcasting first started, most episodes were listened to on a computer. Today, more than 64% of podcasts are listened to on a mobile device.

---

[9] "2019 Podcast Stats & Facts (New Research from June 2019)." Podcast Insights®. Available at https://www.podcastinsights.com/podcast-statistics/.

- Weekly podcast listeners consume seven shows per week on average. This number correlates with the daily activities people engage in, such as gym sessions or while commuting to work. More than 52% of listeners tune in to podcasts while in the car, 46% while travelling on planes, 40% while walking, running and biking, 37% on public transport and 32% when they work out.[10]

Jay Baer, one of the most popular marketing and social media Influencers, says the sweet spot is to publish a podcast episode five times per week. However, in my experience, and after speaking with Australian audiences, people find this a little noisy. By starting with just one podcast episode per week, you'll be ahead of the game!

Kinaesthetic Content – Create a Video

There's no doubt that video is one of the most powerful ways to get your content in front of people. From Facebook Lives to YouTube, more videos are being consumed than ever before.

According to drop shipping marketing company, Oberlo[11]:

- 85% of internet users in the US watch video content every month.

- 54% of people want to see more video content from a brand they trust.

---

10 "The Podcast Audience." Why Podcasts. Available at http://www.whypodcasts.org/audience/.

11 Mohsin, Maryam (13 January 2020). "10 Video Marketing Statistics That You Need to Know in 2020 [Infographic]." Oberlo. Available at https://au.oberlo.com/blog/video-marketing-statistics.

- 87% of marketers recommend video as a marketing tool. Videos are a consumer's favourite content type.

- 88% of marketers say they're happy with the ROI for video.

- Video marketers get 66% more leads than non-video marketers.

- The average user spends 88% more time on a website if it has video than without.

- Eight out of 10 people have purchased a product after watching a brand's video.

- Internet users spent six hours and 48 minutes each week watching videos online in 2019.

- In 2022 it's expected that 82% of the world's internet traffic will come from video streaming and downloads.

There's no doubt about it, video works because it builds trust. And it's not going anywhere!

In fact, videoing your piece of content first can actually be quicker than writing it out, or transcribing it first. It just takes a bit of practice. Julian Mather, the author of Get Video Smart and an expert in creating video for business, says to fully take advantage of video, you need to do the following[12]:

---

12 Mather, Julian (undated). "How To Script, Shoot, Edit and Caption Your First LinkedIn Video in One Hour at No Cost." Available at https://www.julianmather.com/blog/how-to-make-your-first-linkedin-video.

1. Write Your script (which can come from the transcription of your content page).

2. Get your lighting right. Natural light is best so facing a window can be helpful.

3. Add captions. (Plenty of people out there can help with this. Check out sites like Fivver and Upwork.)

4. Load your video!

Cadence - Find your rhythm

When creating content, find a rhythm that works for you. You may find early mornings work best, or once-per-week blocks, working in the cracks, two-day retreats, or capturing content on the go. Once you find your cadence, you'll find your flow, and once you find your flow, your content and ideas will start to come to life rather than sit in your head. It becomes like turning on the tap — when you need them, your content and ideas flow out easily.

As actor *William Shatner* said, "Your cadence is your music." I think that's so true. Music is a creative expression, and when you can find your creative expression through your ideas, it really is your music.

I remember **working with Jess**. She was a marketing consultant and mother of two young boys under four. She lived about an hour and a half outside of the city and was getting very busy. She still could only really work two to three days a week, including time for content creation.

So, what we had to do was find the cadence and rhythm for her lifestyle. Jess had to do quite a bit of driving to the city to meet clients, so she needed to make use of that time in her car. She would make a list of her ideas, then write them down. Each idea usually took about 10 minutes to create before getting in the car. She would talk through her ideas on the way to meet her clients and record them on her phone, then use a transcription service like www.rev.com. In fact, she created most of her social media content in the car.

> **Mihaly Csikszentmihalyi,** author of the book *Flow,* says you need to identify your creative flow to help you feel fulfilled. This sense of flow also makes the time go fast, so it doesn't feel like it's a labourious, challenging or frustrating process.

Here are some steps you can take to find your flow. This is the process I teach most of my clients and have had the best success with:

1. **Catch the idea:** Tools like Memo Mailer (which we talked about in Chapter 4) are great. You could also keep a notepad in your car or handbag to unpack your ideas. Take a photo of them and make sure you have a file to store your ideas. I personally keep folders of topics with Word documents in each, so when it's time to develop or work on an idea, I'm not sitting around wondering when a great idea will come along.

② **Block time:** Once you have captured your ideas, you need block time in your calendar to sit down and unpack them. So, you need a system to unpack the idea, and then you need time to create it. You could block time in your calendar on a Friday morning or whenever works for you. What's important is that you set up a cadence and rhythm so you make use of your ideas. You don't want them to come along just to be forgotten.

Your ideas are the most valuable resource you have to lead, innovate and drive change.

Become Prolific - The Intersection of Strategy and Creativity

Finding a creative way to share ideas and messages can be challenging. Creativity takes vulnerability. Many of us fear our ideas being rejected. Fundamentally, we all want to be part of a community and have a strong sense of belonging. But when we create and put ourselves out there, we risk judgement. One of the first ways to overcome our fear of being judged is to stop judging ourselves.

New York Times best-selling author and expert in shame, connection and vulnerability, *Brené Brown*, says vulnerability is *"the core of shame and fear and our struggle for worthiness. But it appears it's also the birthplace of joy, of creativity, of belonging and love."*[13]

What holds us back is fear of the rejection of our tribe and community. We have a primal fear of being ostracised and "left to die" that stems from our most basic instincts. We are afraid that if we aren't good enough, we will no longer be accepted by others.

But letting go of this fear and allowing ourselves to be creative are critical for us to survive and thrive as leaders.

The Institute for the Future has identified 10 key work skills needed in the future of work. These are :[14]

1. **Sensemaking:** The ability to translate information, data and insights into easy to understand information for audiences.

2. **Novel and Adaptive Thinking:** The ability to shift, pivot and cope with change through innovation.

3. **Social Intelligence:** Understanding human behaviour and motivation for why people do what they do.

4. **Transdisciplinary:** The ability to understand concepts across multiple disciplines.

5. **New Media Literacy:** The ability to present and share information in a way where people can learn more easily by using a variety of platforms.

6. **Computational Thinking:** The ability to translate vast amounts of data into abstract concepts and to understand data-based reasoning.

7. **Cognitive Load Management:** The ability to deal with overwhelm, too much information and decision fatigue.

---

13 Brown, B. (2010). "The power of vulnerability." TEDxHouston. Available at https://www.ted.com/talks/brene_brown_on_vulnerability.

14 Institute for the Future. "Future Work Skills 2020." Available at http://www.iftf.org/futureworkskills/.

8. **Cross Cultural Competency:** The ability to operate in different cultural settings.

9. **Design Mindset:** The ability to represent and develop tasks and work processes to achieve desired outcomes.

10. **Virtual Collaboration:** The ability to work productively, drive engagement, and demonstrate presence as a member of a virtual team.

These 10 key skills allow change agents the ability to creatively communicate ideas and have influence.

So, how can you achieve this?

1. **Know your audience:** Think about your audience and who you're speaking to.

2. **Create variety:** Use different media to communicate your message – for example, a podcast or video. You could use different cuts of video, or do a video on location somewhere while you're travelling. You've got to find different locations, different ways of telling stories and different ways to get information in front of people. Entrepreneur Gary Vee is worth checking out. He doesn't just do a lot of videos; he uses many different ways to communicate his messages.
Use metaphors: People can grasp information and complex

3. ideas when you put them in a format that's familiar and easy for people to understand.

Questions for you from here

1. **Choose** one of your 50 things lists.

2. **Ensure you have** the Content Page tool (you can download it here: https://janeandersonspeaks.com/catalystcontentresources

3. **Unpack your ideas** into one page of content (your content page) with a key message, opinion, story, research, metaphor, quote and steps. Number the piece of content so you know how many you have created. The goal is to create 100 per year.

4. **Transcribe** your piece of content using a tool like www.rev.com or another transcription service. You should receive your transcription back within a few minutes.

5. **If you're stuck** on a story think about which one of the five STAR stories you could use.

6. **Undertake research** based on the content.

7. **Block time** in your calendar to create your content page based on your cadence, routines and flow (daily, weekly, monthly, quarterly or yearly etc.).

6
DISTRIBUTION

"Content is king, but distribution is the queen. She wears the pants."
Jonah Peretti, CEO Buzz feed

Whilst it is one thing to create content, it's quite another to distribute it. For most of the clients I work with, this is the biggest shift they need to make to grow their message, positioning and influence. Most see all three activities – ideation, creation and distribution – as one activity, and this perception slows the whole process down.

Another problem arises when clients try to outsource the creation of the content. While this is a good idea in theory, in reality it often means their content comes across as inauthentic and lacking personality. It becomes white noise, invisible and powerless. The key is to outsource the **distribution** of the content rather than the content creation.

Great distribution requires a foundation of great systems. So, let's start there!

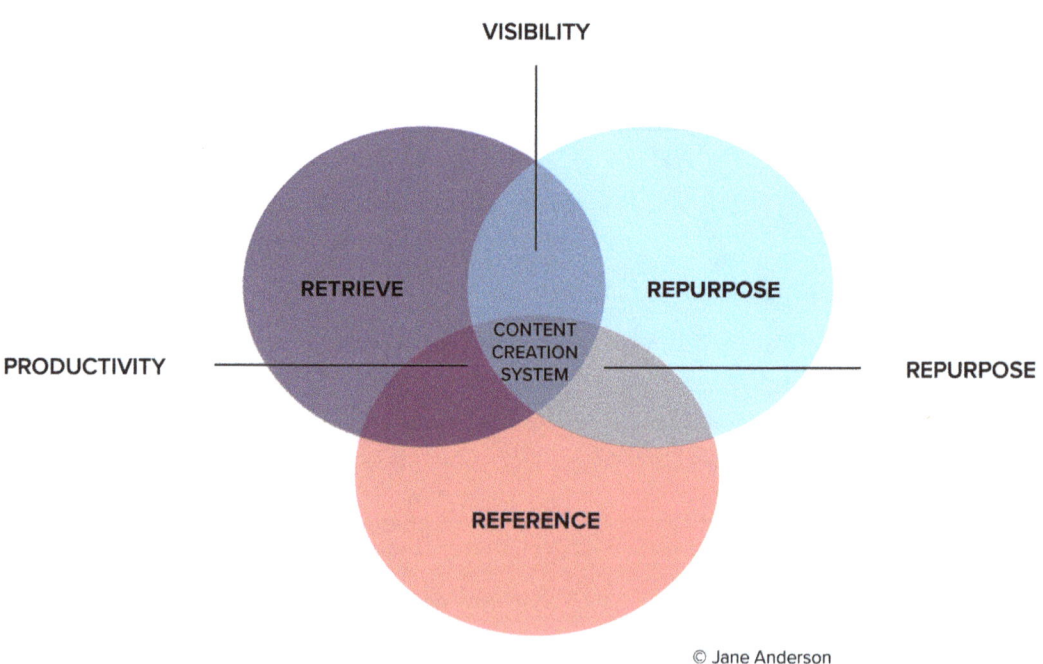

© Jane Anderson

At one point in my life I wanted to be a librarian. I love books and reading and discovering new ideas. And I always found myself fascinated by the cataloguing of information and the rapid way a librarian could put their hands on any book, anywhere in the library.

I never did become a librarian, but when I went to work for a productivity company I was able to help people manage their file systems so they were better able to access information for easy retrieval and reference. In a way, I was a productivity 'librarian'!

When capturing your ideas and unpacking your knowledge, you need to have good systems in place to be able to retrieve, repurpose and reference your work easily. Having a system for your content creation is a bit like running a library.

There are **three things** you need to have in your content creation file structure system:

1. **Retrieve:** Having a good file structure and being able to find your content easily saves you a lot of time. Kerry Gleeson in his book, The Personal Efficiency Program, found that the average person spends over six weeks per year trying to find things. We need to make sure that you're not trying to find information, but that you know where it is and can put your hands on it quickly.

2. **Repurpose:** You need to be able to repurpose your content easily. If you can repurpose it, then you can maximise the potential of each piece of content. In fact, many of our clients will repurpose one piece of content about 40 times to maximise the use out of it.

3. **Reference:** A big part of being able to communicate effectively is being able to reference key pieces of research or work that's already been done in the space.

If you can get your retrieval and repurposing working, then you'll increase the amount of content that goes out and you'll increase your visibility. At the intersection of repurposing and referencing your IP quickly, you'll increase your credibility and trust as a leader. And if you can retrieve and reference your IP quickly, you're going to improve your own productivity, which will ultimately increase your influence and drive change.

As *Mike Michalowicz* who wrote the New York Times best-selling book, The Big Pumpkin Idea, said, *"Systems don't simplify the results, systems simplify the process of getting there."*

To access a video about filing your content for easy retrieval and reference, go to

[https://janeandersonspeaks.com/catalystcontentresources.](https://janeandersonspeaks.com/catalystcontentresources)

You'll also see you have access to a spreadsheet to catalogue your content so you know where you're up to in your content creation and can keep track of your IP.

Once you have your content stored easily, then it's time to leverage it across multiple platforms for business growth. Many think that social media is the only platform, but let's look at a contextual framework before we talk about social media specifically.

Leveraging your content for lead generation

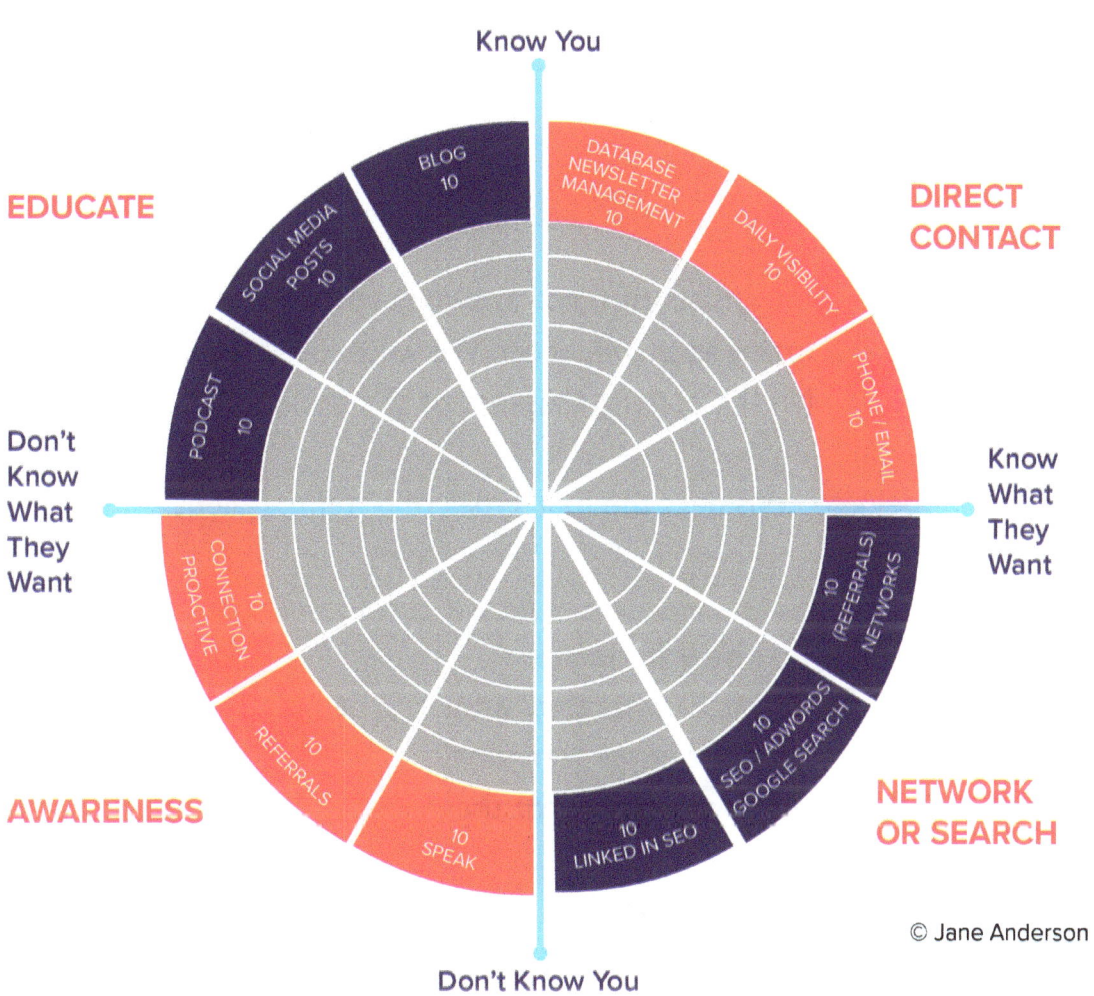

The Lead Generation for Thought Leaders model provides you with real, actionable steps to take you from entrepreneur to Influencer. It will ensure that people not only find you, but want to work with you.

The model contains the following four quadrants:

- Direct Contact
- Network or Search
- Awareness
- Educate

Each quadrant consists of three activities you must undertake to build your positioning as an Influencer. We will explain these activities in further detail in the coming chapters of this book.

The model also considers the four types of potential clients out there:

- People who know someone.
- People who know what they want.
- People who don't know someone.
- People who don't know what they want.

Let's examine these four types of consumer and how they relate to the different quadrants of the model.

Direct Contact

"I know someone who can help me and I know what I want."

This type of customer already knows who you are. They know that you offer what they need. But for them to take that next step and call you or email you, you must be at the front of their mind. So, it's important you keep in regular contact.

As an *Influencer,* you will generally need to communicate at least once per week until you have solid footing in your market. Solid footing would be when you're turning over around $650,000 plus per year. Anything below that, or if you are accessing a new type of client, will mean you need to really ramp up your communication.

Most don't communicate enough and are afraid of annoying people or being spammy. They are also worried about people unsubscribing if they are seen as communicating too much. Many Influencers in the US communicate almost daily, or three times per week via email and isn't unusual.

For example, *Nikki Fogden-Moore* is an expert in vitality and is based on the Sunshine Coast in Queensland, Australia. She specialises in working with super-busy executives and entrepreneurs who are tired, lacking energy and balance. She sends them an email each Monday called her "Monday Mojo". It's a great email to receive first thing each week and puts a spring in the receiver's step.

Building your client database is critical to keeping in touch. Your database can include existing clients, people you've met or groups of people with a common interest or problem. You need to reach out to your database regularly to maintain visibility. The idea is that you come immediately to mind when they need you, or when someone they know needs someone like you.

Direct contact is the most valuable quadrant of the model. Building your client database requires plenty of groundwork and you must keep at it day in, day out. But the benefits are enormous. As American entrepreneur *Seth Godin*, best-selling author of Tribes, says: "The people who will buy from you are those who know you."

Network or Search

"I don't know someone who can help me, but I know what I want."

In this situation, the potential client will seek recommendations. If they're extroverted or well-networked, they will consult their colleagues and friends for referrals as they trust them. If they're more introverted, they will conduct an online search. Sometimes people will do both.

Being referred by a network is ideal. It means you have a good reputation, and when you have a good reputation, you have solid positioning. It makes your job of finding new clients so much easier. Knowing who your current and potential key referrers are is crucial. Once you know who they are you can apply specific strategies to reward and encourage them more.

A good example of this is an insolvency firm we recently worked with. This field of financial planners, accountants, insolvency specialists and lawyers can often be very complicated and requires a high level of knowledge. Often the average consumer won't know what to do if their business were to become insolvent.

So, instead of going straight to an insolvency firm, the consumer's first port of call will usually be their lawyer or their accountant who will then refer them onto the insolvency firm. *Most* business owners won't go directly to an insolvency agency as it's so specialised. This high level of specialisation means they're really known for knowing something, and when they are needed, they are easily found and referred to. You want to be become like an insolvency firm – specialised, respected and easily referred to.

Being found on the first page of a Google search result is often seen as the nirvana of business growth. But for an Influencer's practice it's entirely different as the potential client doing the search doesn't know you. No one has referred you, so it's difficult for you to stand out. You'll be competing with other people and businesses who also come up in the search – some of whom may have more experience with search engine optimisation and Google AdWords than you, so they will appear higher in the results list. And the higher someone is in the results list, the more likely the potential client will click on their link.

In a Google search you look very similar to everybody else – rather like toothpaste on a supermarket shelf. It's hard to sell your defining features and uniqueness. Without craft copywriting and heavy SEO work, you're usually competing on price, and that's a difficult space in which to sell.

Whilst your buyer may be ready, you really need to be able to compete aggressively to stand out when you're found. This can be really hard to do when you're an Influencer. Nevertheless, it's important that we discuss it so you know where it fits in the Influencer business growth process.

But if you are well networked, your referrals will come to the fore – even in search engine results. If you don't have a LinkedIn profile, set one up now! Ultimately, LinkedIn is a search engine, so it's essential that you set up your LinkedIn profile with the right keywords. That way, you'll be more likely to turn up in online search results.

Awareness

"I don't know someone who can help me and I don't know what I want."

This activity is designed to access new markets as they don't know you and they may not have come across your insights or thinking or articulated the problems that you're able to solve. Ignorance can be bliss in this quadrant, so you have to be able to penetrate the noise they're exposed to in order to grasp their attention.

To engage this type of client, you need to build awareness. Awareness of who you are, what you do, who you help and how you help. Blog posts, articles, videos, podcasts and social media profiles are all important tools in your awareness arsenal.

The work you do offline is important, too. Public speaking, attending networking events and appearing at expos will help your potential clients get to know you. They will see that while they may not need your help right now, down the track they – or someone they know – may have a problem they need you to solve. The goal is to continually be proactive and reach out to others so you can grow your list and start to nurture them.

A great example of this is a client we recently worked with called Adam. He's an expert in creating high performing schools and learning cultures. He's been so successful that he's taken his approach to the corporate market to help corporate organisations that are struggling under the same problems. But doing this was like starting his business all over again. We had to help him access those people who didn't know they had these problems and didn't know Adam. He had to be super-proactive in reaching out to connect and start educating them on his message.

Advertising, PR and radio are all valuable activities here, but in an Influencer world your list is everything. You need to ensure all roads maximise the opportunity to build list, not live in hope that they will need help immediately, which is usually not the case.

A great example of someone who does this and is very particular about it is Elon Musk, the CEO of Tesla and SpaceX. In fact, he's renowned for going through PR consultants who don't grasp and execute his vision. He realises the value of this quadrant in trying to raise awareness with people who don't know him or his message of creating a sustainable planet on a massive global scale.

Educate

"I know who can help me but I don't know what I want."

Although they know who you are, these kinds of customers are not aware that they need your help. In this case, it is your job to educate them. You must regularly create and share content so people understand what you do. By educating them on how you can help them, they may realise they have a problem – but they just weren't aware of it until now. People often do not realise they have an issue they need resolving or an area they could improve on unless someone educates them.

Writing posts, sharing updates and providing insightful comments are simple ways to educate and demonstrate your deep understanding of the problems you solve. The goal of your content is to encourage your audience to think, "Wow, that's exactly what I'm after!" It must provide a clear connection between their problems and your solutions.

> It's easy to take the Influencer Indicator to identify how to leverage your content to activate your marketing and lead generation gaps. It's normally $80 to buy but if you follow this link it's yours for free.
>
> https://janeandersonspeaks.com/Influencer-indicator

A specific comment on social media distribution

Social media has completely transformed consumer and service provider interaction. It has put everyone on a level playing field; small businesses have as much clout as large corporations, and consumers have a direct, public channel of communication with the businesses they deal with.

Facebook, LinkedIn, Twitter, Instagram, Pinterest, YouTube – the list of social networking platforms goes on. Facebook alone has 1.63 billion daily active users around the globe[1].

If you want to educate your audience, generate leads and clinch more sales, it's a no-brainer – you need to be seen on social media.

In my work, I often meet people who feel overwhelmed by social media. They're hesitant to post their own content. I'm often told, "I don't know what to write. I don't want people to think I'm cocky or arrogant." Or, "What if people don't agree with what I post? What if they say negative things about me? I don't think I could cope!"

The tall poppy syndrome has a lot to answer for. In Australian culture, it's undesirable to stand out from the crowd. People shy away from the spotlight, fearing others will think they're egotistical. This fear extends to social media, where entrepreneurs choose the safe option of only sharing other people's content – or nothing at all.

---

1 Facebook Company Information. Available at http://newsroom.fb.com/company-info/.

But your potential clients and existing customers want to hear from you. Figures from LinkedIn show that six out of every 10 users are interested in industry insights[2] . This means your audience wants to be educated about your area of expertise and perspective.
LinkedIn goes on to say: *"Your followers are active on LinkedIn because they want to be more productive and successful professionals. Informative, useful updates receive the highest engagement rates because that's the information members expect from companies they follow on LinkedIn."*

Previously, only elite, invitation-only Influencers could post their own original content on LinkedIn. Now, anyone can. Yet, only 1% of the 500 million people with a LinkedIn profile do[3] . This represents an enormous opportunity for you to reach and educate your target audience with your content.

To have maximum impact with social media, you need to take a three-dimensional approach. The below model explains how this works.

---

[2] Lee, K. (2014). "7 Essential LinkedIn Marketing Stats: When to Post, What to Post and How to Improve." *The Next Web*. Available at https://thenextweb.com/socialmedia/2014/04/04/7-essential-linkedin-stats-post-post-improve/.

[3] Roth, D. (2015). More Than 1 Million Members are Now Publishing on LinkedIn." LinkedIn. Available at https://blog.linkedin.com/2015/07/09/1-million-linkedin-publishers.

Three-Dimensional Social Media for Experts

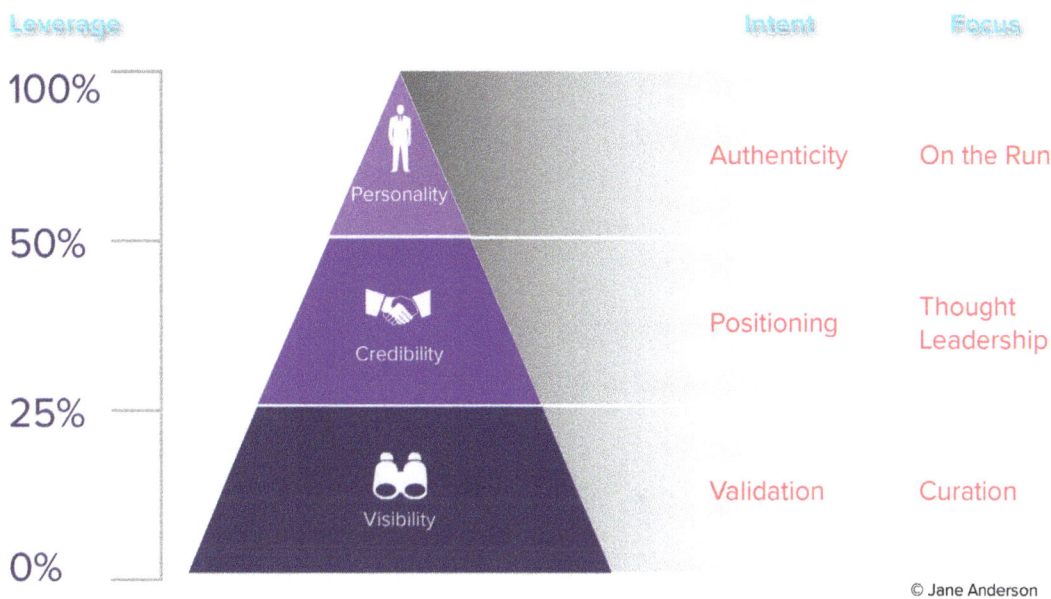

To establish an effective, three-dimensional social media strategy, you need to work your way through each of the following levels:

Level 1 : Visibility

At this level, you're trying to establish a consistent online presence. You're focused on content **curation** – sharing the expertise of others to **validate** your message and positioning. You're posting at least once a day to familiarise people with your face and your message.

As an entrepreneur, your face and your message are two of your most important assets. You need be visible, however, it's important that the information you share aligns with both your message and your audience's needs.

As US sales expert *Harvey Mackay* once said, *"Don't confuse visibility with credibility."* Visibility is about supporting your clients. Posting regular content doesn't necessarily mean you're educating or elevating your positioning. But you can achieve greater visibility if the information you share is relevant to your audience and validates what you're trying to say.

The amount of leverage you can receive from your social media strategy at this level is about 25% of what's possible.

Level 2 : Credibility

Once you've established your visibility, you need to work on your credibility. Credibility is what gives your **positioning** its strength. Without credibility, everything you say and do is meaningless.

This level is about demonstrating that you're an authority in your industry. Sharing your own case studies, research and original ideas will cement your positioning as a **thought leader.**

The amount of leverage you can receive at this level is about 50% of what's possible from your social media strategy.

Level 3 : Personality

Now that you've achieved visibility and have proven your credibility, you need to focus on your personality. Sharing your personality with your audience establishes your **authenticity.** It gives you flavour and uniqueness. People want to see the person behind the message; it helps them connect with you more easily.

In the words of *Walt Disney*, *"Until a character becomes a personality, it cannot be believed.... Without personality, a story cannot ring true to the audience."*

At this top level, you'll want to make the most of opportunities to share your personality **on the run**. For example, if you've attended an event, spoken at a conference or had something interesting happen to you that day, post about it!

The amount of leverage you can receive at this level is 100% of what's possible.

Bear in mind that you can't skip straight from level one to level three. Don't pressure yourself. Take the time to master each level so you build a solid online presence. Only once you have built your visibility and credibility can you work on the personality of your social media strategy.

Content Curation

Content curation is not only an efficient way for you to create social media posts, it bolsters your authenticity, too. Content creation is the process of collecting information relevant to your area of expertise and presenting it in a meaningful way. Compiling and sharing existing content from respected sources adds value for your followers. It shows them that you genuinely want to educate them. It also adds weight to your own message – if someone else has said it, it's more trustworthy.

There are four main reasons why content curation works:

1. **It validates your message.** If you can show that other experts share your views, your audience is more likely to trust and respect you.

2. **You can contrast your insights.** Sharing views you disagree with means you can add your expertise and insights to the conversation.

3. **It's less salesy.** When you share other people's insights and research, you're less likely to come across as self-promoting in your posts.

4. **It's efficient.** You'll spend less time writing content, which means you can share more, add more value and increase your visibility.

The ideal content ratio

"You give before you get."
Napoleon Hill

Content curation combined with your own thought leadership is powerful. But you need to get the ratio right. The ideal content ratio is 80:20 if you don't have enough original content. That is, 80% of the content you share should be curated.

The remaining 20% should be your original content. As an Influencer, you want to advance the thinking around your subject. But you don't want to over-expose your audience to your ideas. Limiting your own content to 20% of what you post reduces your risk of looking like a second-hand car dealer. You'll be able to highlight your offerings and educate your audience without making them feel as though they're being sold to all the time.

Create a content plan

To keep your message on track, a content plan is essential. You need to be clear about your goals to ensure your content plan is strategic. What do you want to sell this quarter? What are your goals for the next quarter? Plan your content around these goals.

It's a great idea to write your social media content 12 to 18 months in advance. All you need is a spreadsheet. If you don't plan, generating content each day becomes a real struggle. With a solid content plan in place, you will know exactly what you need to say and when.

When planning your content, there are several time-saving tools available to you. Feedspot is a fabulous way to share content — and it's free. Once you set up your account, choose a word related to your area of expertise — for example, the word "resilience". Feedspot will send you a weekly email with links to articles it has found related to resilience. Use these links to create your social media posts.

Post Frequency

How often should you post on social media? Finding the right balance can be tricky. On the one hand, if you post too often, you could irritate your audience. You'll clog up their newsfeeds and they'll unfollow you. On the other hand, if you don't post enough, your audience will forget you. You'll lose traction with your personal brand and positioning. So, how can you get it just right?

The answer depends on several factors: the social media platforms you use, your industry, your business goals and your audience, to name a few.

But there are some general rules of thumb you can use as a blueprint. Social media-sharing platform Buffer suggests the following guide :[3]

▶ **Pinterest: 5+ times per day.** Top brands have said they experience rapid growth by posting multiple times a day.

---

[3] Lee, K. (2015). "Infographic: How Often Should You Post on Social Media? See the Most Popular Research and Tips." *Buffer*. Available at https://blog.bufferapp.com/how-often-post-social-media.

- **Twitter: 24+ times per day.** Engagement slightly decreases after a third tweet.

- **Facebook: 2 posts per day.** Any more than this and the number of likes and comments decreases.

- **Instagram: 2 posts per day.** Major brands post an average of 2 times per day to Instagram.

What about LinkedIn? Its own research has found that 20 posts per month can help you reach 60% of your unique audience[4]. This works out to be one post every weekday for four weeks. If you have the time and the quality content, try scaling up your number of LinkedIn posts to reap more benefits.

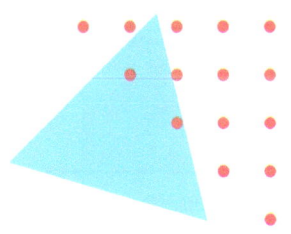

---

4 Lua, A. (2015). "The Quick Guide to LinkedIn Marketing Strategy: 9 Best Practices." *Buffer.* Available at https://buffer.com/library/linkedin-marketing.

The variety of social media platforms ◆

◆ *LinkedIn*

LinkedIn is a social network of more than 610 million people[5], from CEOs to frontline staff, across a broad range of industries. It is a search algorithm based on networks and keywords. LinkedIn has created a complex algorithm of search tools and other platforms within it to enhance the experience. It also has an advertising platform.

LinkedIn is a little like an online resume, in that you can list your current and previous roles, create a blog, advertise a job and reach out to your ideal clients.

According to LinkedIn:

- Professionals are signing up to join LinkedIn at a rate of more than two new members per second.[6]

- There are more than 40 million students and recent college graduates on LinkedIn. They are LinkedIn's fastest-growing demographic.[7]

---

5 Hutchinson, A. (2019). "LinkedIn Reaches 610 Million Members, Publishes New eBook on Social Media Management Tips." *Social Media Today*. Available at https://www.socialmediatoday.com/news/linkedin-reaches-610-million-members-publishes-new-ebook-on-social-media/547620/.

6 Statistics. LinkedIn Newsroom. Available at https://news.linkedin.com/about-us#statistics.

7 Corona, B. (2017). "LinkedIn Statistics Every B2B Company Needs to Know for Marketing & Recruitment Strategy." Blue Corona. Available at https://www.bluecorona.com/blog/linkedin-stats.

◆ *Facebook*

Facebook has more than 2.41 billion monthly active users as of August 31, 2019.[8] As of April 2020, Facebook was the most popular social networking site in the world[9], based on the number of active user accounts.

Facebook is often used for business-to-consumer marketing activity. As a practice, you can have a personal page and a business page, with Facebook's marketing favouring business pages that pay for advertising.

Many business owners find Facebook's advertising platform complicated. It's easy to waste money with no results, so I recommend you seek the help of a Facebook advertising expert to help you.

◆ *Twitter*

Twitter posts – or tweets – were previously limited to 140 characters, but in 2017 Twitter expanded this to 280 characters[10]. Tweets are based on conversations and hashtags to make the content searchable. With only 280 characters to work with, it's a great way to learn how to be succinct with your message!

---

8 "Number of monthly active Facebook users worldwide as of 2nd quarter 2019." (2019). Statista. Available at https://www.statista.com/statistics/264810/number-of-monthly-active-facebook-users-worldwide/.
9 Ibid.

10 Perez, S. (2017). "Twitter officially expands its character count to 280 starting today." Tech Crunch. Available at https://techcrunch.com/2017/11/07/twitter-officially-expands-its-character-count-to-280-starting-today/.

Twitter has more than 330 million monthly active users,[11] and 82% are active users on mobile.[12] Furthermore, 79% of Twitter accounts are based outside the United States.[13]

In recent years, Twitter has declined in popularity. It's trying to reinvent itself to keep up with changing social media trends.

◆ *Instagram*

Instagram is one of the most powerful social media platforms. It's the only social media platform that almost guarantees your profile a spot at the top of the feed. That's because Instagram has a feature called Stories.

Stories brings your brand to life. It allows you to share and collate multiple photos and videos; all the moments of your day that combine to create your unique "story".

Videos are invaluable when it comes to building your personal brand. Gary Vee says spontaneous videos are an effective form of documentation. They capture your thoughts as they happen and help you collate your unique content – vital for any Influencer.

So, it's no surprise that Stories is proving to be a crucial brand-building tool for Influencers. Recent data shows that while Facebook has the highest number of members in Australia, Instagram is the

---

[11] "Number of monthly active Twitter users worldwide from 1st quarter 2010 to 1st quarter 2019." (2019). Statista. Available at https://www.statista.com/statistics/282087/number-of-monthly-active-twitter-users/.

[12] Pestov, I. (2016). "Today's Incredible Numbers About Social Media." *Medium*. Available at https://medium.com/@ipestov/todays-incredible-numbers-about-social-media-a6b1ff2ca887.

[13] "Twitter by the Numbers: Stats, Demographics & Fun Facts." (2019). Omnicore. Available at https://www.omnicoreagency.com/twitter-statistics/.

fastest-growing social network.[14] Since Stories launched in 2016, there's also been a decline in Snapchat usage[15] – previously the only social media platform that allowed users to post videos "on the run".

What's more, Instagram is driven by hashtags. This means it acts like a search engine, so you're more likely to turn up in search results when someone is looking for a business like yours. It also uses location data, which is great news if you're targeting an audience in a specific area – for example, if you are a personal trainer in Brisbane.

There are **two ways** you can use Instagram to your advantage:

1. **As a polished branding tool.**
Stylised images and videos can give your brand a refined edge.

2. **As a spontaneous capture tool.**
Videos allow you to share the moments of your day as they happen. They give your audience a unique insight in to who you are, what you do and how you can help them. It also shows them that you're a "real" person, not simply a message.

Negotiation expert Tony Perzow[16] is a fantastic example of someone who uses Instagram videos in a powerful way. His videos not only market his programs, they also inform, entertain and educate his audience. Wholehearted Studio's Hayley Jenkin[17] is another entrepreneur who uses Instagram exceptionally well. Her

---

14 (January 1, 2017). "Social Media Statistics Australia – December 2016." SocialMediaNews.com.au. Available at https://www.socialmedianews.com.au/social-media-statistics-australia-december-2016/.

15 (January 30, 2017). "Instagram's Stories is stealing Snapchat's users." TechCrunch. Available at https://techcrunch.com/2017/01/30/attack-of-the-clone/.

16 Available at https://www.instagram.com/tony_perzow/.

17 Available at https://www.instagram.com/wholeheartedstudio/.

images and videos are more stylised and consciously crafted, which is perfect for building her photography business' sophisticated brand.

Entrepreneurs often have a fear of appearing inauthentic or "showy". Social media can be a real struggle for them, so they play it safe and do nothing. Consequently, their competitors appear at the top of their audiences' social media feeds. They're the ones who make an impact and get the leads.

Be fearless. To be an Influencer and share your content, you must embrace social media. Don't get hung up about appearing perfect – people want to see the real you. Videos can give you enormous cut through with your audience. Better yet, you don't need to spend vast amounts of money or have a professional recording studio. In this regard, Instagram is a perfect ally.

◆ Snapchat

Snapchat is a photo and video-messaging app. Launched in 2011, Snapchat is unique in that all images and videos last only a brief amount of time before they disappear forever. This makes the app ephemeral in nature, although you can take a screenshot of all the snaps you receive to save them in picture form. You can also save your own snaps before sending them to friends or posting them via Stories.

> As of **September 2019,** the app's users were sending three billion snaps a day.[18] Due to the instant popularity of Snapchat, Facebook reportedly offered to acquire it for $3 billion.[19] But the cash offer was declined. Facebook later launched a similar app, called Slingshot, but it failed to catch on.

Snapchat is mostly a hit among teenagers and people in their 20s, according to several research firms. But it is catching on and being embraced by new demographics every day. YouTubers and celebrities are all known to use Snapchat as an alternative for communicating with their followers.

◆ TikTok

TikTok is the new kid on the block. It allows users to create and share short-form videos, such as short lip-sync, comedy and talent videos. The social media app was launched in 2017 by Chinese developer ByteDance for markets outside of China. It's still in its early days, but is rapidly gaining momentum. TikTok requires native content to be posted, so, in other words, there is no facility to schedule content to increase efficiency.

A common question from people who have identified the best social media platforms for their content is, "How do I increase efficiency with posting?" It is possible to use third-party applications, such as Buffer, Later and Hootsuite. However, keep in mind that social media platforms don't prioritise content from scheduled apps.

Currently, Facebook Business pages are the only social media platform with a scheduling tool for native content. But, while you might increase your efficiency with third-party scheduling apps, you will lose cut-through. Some of the biggest Influencer brands like Gary Vee have teams that undertake native posting, and that's why they gain such a following with their large volume of content.

---

18 "Snapchat by the Numbers: Stats, Demographics & Fun Facts." (2019). Omnicore. Available at https://www.omnicoreagency.com/snapchat-statistics/.

19 Bercovici, Jeff (November 13, 2013). "Facebook Tried to Buy Snapchat for $3B in Cash. Here's Why." *Forbes*, Available at https://www.forbes.com/sites/jeffbercovici/2013/11/13/facebook-wouldve-bought-snapchat-for-3-billion-in-cash-heres-why/#5526acd143de.

◆ *Newsletter*

To remain visible to your audience and gain their trust, you must send content-rich e-newsletters regularly. Consistency is key. Decide how often you're going to send your e-newsletter — fortnightly, weekly or more, and what time and day of the week you will send it. Stick to your schedule. You want your audience to be able to depend on seeing your email land in their inbox. Even if they don't open every e-newsletter you send, receiving it serves as a regular reminder that you're available when they need you.

Create an e-newsletter content plan. You can plan one month, six months or even 12 months in advance. This ensures you don't run out of ideas. It also keeps the information you share via all your channels of communication consistent.

◆ *Where to from here?*

As you can see, it's easy to help those you already know. It can be hard work reaching out to people you've never met while creating awareness of what you do and building your networks. But all four quadrants on the model on page 107 are crucial to leveraging your content to its maximum potential. And you must work on them every day – not just once or twice a year when you have a spare couple of hours. Everything you do in your business must link to this model.

Remember, there is always someone out there trying to find you – even if they don't know it yet!

Questions for you to answer

1. What distribution channels does your ideal audience hang out on?

   _____
   _____
   _____

2. Which channels would be best to create a sense of omnipresence for your audience?

   _____
   _____
   _____

3. How might you adapt your content to suit those channels?

   _____
   _____
   _____

4. What tools will you use to increase the efficiency of your content distribution?

_____

_____

_____

5. What distribution cycle will you use to ensure your content is repurposed? Can you post a podcast every Wednesday and a blog post every Thursday etc.?

_____

_____

_____

6. Which parts of your content could you outsource for distribution?

_____

_____

_____

7. How will you check your content distribution to ensure it is working?

_____

_____

_____

8. What schedulers could you use to reduce the amount of administration in your distribution? *Hint… look at platforms like Buffer and Hootsuite. If you're using Workplace by Facebook it also has a post scheduler.*

_____

_____

_____

9. What can you do to create daily visibility on your platforms if you don't have enough content? In other words, what will you curate?

_____

_____

_____

10. What aspects of your day-to-day life can you share to bring some of your personality to your content?

_____

_____

_____

In Closing

This book covers a lot of ground from what trust was in the past, to where it is today and its implications for the future of work and growing your business. The concepts in the book are designed to start the conversation and help you begin your journey rather than feel overwhelmed by too much content to create. Consider how the concepts may apply to you, your team and your organisation, as well as build your brand, trust, connection and influence for the people who matter in your world.

The ideas behind this book are designed to help give you a framework to consider, measure and gain insights into areas where you have strengths, and other areas that are an opportunity to focus on and improve. As each area improves, you'll see a continuous levelling up - whether each day, quarter or year - which comes from making more conscious and intentional choices around trust in building your tribe.

The key to remember is not to be afraid to start small. Whilst becoming more prolific with your content may seem like a huge mountain to climb, it starts with you having one conversation, one idea at a time. Take the lead and be the example that others can follow. From there the ripple of change begins.

I would love to hear how you go implementing your ideation, creation and distribution. Please reach out to share your stories and examples to me at

jane@jane-anderson.com.au

Work with Jane

In a world of constant change, there is a greater need for consultants and experts in their fields to lead and help their clients navigate change. To do this they need a highly influential personal brand, catalyst content and effective business support to build their tribe.

With over 20 years experience and as one of the top three branding experts in the world, Jane has helped over 80,000 people to build their identity and influence. She is a certified speaker, on the Forbes Coaches Council and has been featured on Sky Business, The Today Show, The Age, Sydney Morning Herald, BBC and Management Today. The author of seven books, Jane typically speaks at conferences, runs workshops, consults and coaches. She typically helps her clients with the following:

- **Business and Personal Brand Strategy** for Consultants, Thought Leaders, Experts and Influencers
- **Content Creation and Lead Generation** for Consultants, Thought Leaders, Experts, Influencers
- **Influencer Marketing Coach Certification** for Business Coaches and Marketing Consultants
- **Business Manager** for Consultants Certification for Online Business Managers and Virtual Assistants
- **Business Growth Coaching** for Consultants earning $500k-$1.5m in revenue.

Jane holds one of the top 1% viewed LinkedIn profiles and is the host of the "Jane Anderson Show" Podcast where she has interviewed people such as Seth Godin.

She has been nominated for and won numerous industry awards for her expertise including:

- Top three branding Gurus globally
- International Stevie Awards for Coach & Entrepreneur of the Year
- Nominated for Telstra Business Awards 2014, 2016, 2018 and 2019
- Top 25 branding blogs globally
- Top six branding experts in Australia

CORPORATE CLIENTS HAVE INCLUDED:

Telstra, International Rice Research Institute, Wesfarmers, Amadeus, Virgin Australia, IKEA, LEGO, Mercedes-Benz, Australian Medical Association, Shell Energy and Workcover.

> *"Within four weeks of making a couple of modest tweaks, Jane Anderson's advice led to me increasing online revenue by more than $10k! Simple, clear, direct strategies that increase impact and influence."*
>
> — *Dr Justin Coulson,* Parenting Expert

Book in a time to chat here:

- https://calendly.com/jane-0877/complimentary-discussion
- Email: support@jane-anderson.com.au
- Call the office: +61 7 3841 7772

GET INVOLVED

Ideal for Experts, Consultants, Content Creators and Thought Leaders.

Join the club to create 10 pieces of original content in 2 hours every month. The content you create can be repurposed into multiple platforms such as social media, newsletter, whitepaper or your next book.

janeandersonspeaks.com/content-club

Ideal for Experts, Consultants, Content Creators and Thought Leaders.

2-day intensive Content Creation Bootcamp where you undertake "Pomodoro" sprints to complete 50 pieces of content, in other words, 12 months of content.

janeandersonspeaks.com/content-creation-bootcamp

Read more of Jane's Work :

The old ways of growing a business have changed.

Social media has levelled the playing field and now it's easier than ever to compete with the big players in your industry.

Whether you're a Thought Leader, Trusted Advisor, Academic or Expert, the way you position and market yourself is now more important than ever.

This book will help you uncover the 12 secret activities to grow your business and opportunities.

Never has there been an opportunity for businesses and consultants to identify, engage and connect with their ideal audience like there is now with LinkedIn.

By the end of this book, you will have the strategies you need to generate leads and grow your business using LinkedIn.

You will be armed with practical steps that you can implement straight away to see real results. Your outcomes will be stronger, and you will lead the competition on this new playing field.

In a world of disruption and constant change, organisations and their leaders at all levels are being asked to be more transparent, authentic and credible than ever.

In this book, Jane covers the nine key skills of high trust brands and global Influencers that lead with influence and communicate during change.

We're no longer in the industrial or information age. We're now in the connection economy. Companies and governments want innovation, ideas and networks to thrive in volatile economic times. Hard work alone doesn't cut it anymore.

Discover how to create "corporation you" without being a tall poppy to build your Personal Brand.

We all hate selling ourselves, but interviews are one of those times when you can't be shy. You have to stand out from the crowd. From this book, you will learn techniques to increase your confidence, as well as how to anticipate the questions the panel might ask and how to practice in the lead-up to the big day.

www.ingramcontent.com/pod-product-compliance
Lightning Source LLC
Chambersburg PA
CBHW061137010526
44107CB00069B/2972